HISTORY OF

# Regent Street

Hermione Hobhouse

**Macdonald and Jane's, London**
in association with Queen Anne Press, London

ISBN (hard) 0362 00234 7
ISBN (paper) 0362 00236 3

Designed by Pete Pengilley

First published in 1975 by Macdonald and Jane's Ltd,
Paulton House, 8 Shepherdess Walk, London, N1 7LE
in association with Queen Anne Press Ltd,
12 Vandy Street, London, EC2A 2EN.
Printed in Great Britain
by Fletcher & Son, Norwich



**Front cover illustration:** Regent Street looking south from the Hanover Chapel in 1842

**Back cover illustration:** The premises of the Ford Motor Company in 1935 as decorated for the Silver Jubilee of King George V.

# Acknowledgements

It would be impossible to undertake a work of this nature without help from denizens of Regent Street, past and present, and I am deeply indebted to all the firms and individuals who have answered my queries and provided material for research and for reproduction. I am particularly grateful to Patricia Hayward-Ellen, Executive Director of the Regent Street Association, who has given me a great deal of help over all aspects of this book. Others to whom I am indebted include Mr Airey of Airey and Wheeler, Mr Rule of Austin Reed, Miss Phillips of Aquascutum, Mr Thompson of Carringtons, Miss Storr of Dickins and Jones, David Burgess Wise of the Ford Motor Company, Mr Summers of Garrards, Miss Lines of Hamleys, Mr Grilli of Hedges and Butler, Mr Ron Mills of Higgs and Hill, Miss Phillips of Libertys, and Mr Desmond of Lillywhites, Mr Bishop of Mappin and Webb, Miss Suzie Biggs of Trust Houses Forte, and Mrs Raven of Swan and Edgar. I have also been helped by representatives of the Café Royal, Verrey's Restaurant, St George's Hotel, Veeraswamy's Restaurant, Acuman, Lawleys, Jaeger, Scott Adie, Arthur Ackermann, C. Packer, Ciro Pearls, Linguaphone and Negretti and Zambra.

The Crown Estate Commissioners are the landlords of most of Regent Street and they have kindly allowed me to use their records and have given me a good deal of help generally.

I am indebted to Mr Warner of the British Broadcasting Corporation for arranging for me to see over the Langham Hotel, now offices of the BBC.

I am indebted to Penguin Books for permission to quote from Mollie Panter-Downes' *London War Notes* published in 1972 and to Weidenfeld and Nicholson for permission to quote from Leonard Mosley's *Backs to the Wall*, published in 1971.

Like all members, I am much indebted to the London Library whose staff have been invariably helpful and whose indulgence over borrowing I have found, like M. Guizot, a 'great convenience'. I must also express my thanks to the staff of the Westminster Public Library, particularly Miss Swarbrick of the Westminster Local History Collection, and Mr Bowden of the Marylebone Local History Collection, and to Mr Howgego and Mr Hyde of the Guildhall Library. Mr Nicholas Cooper of the National Monuments Record has given me a great deal of help in tracking down illustrations, as have Mr Phillips of the Greater London Council Map Collection, and Miss Watson of the G.L.C. Photograph Library, and the staff of the Department of Prints and Drawings of the British Museum.

I have received general advice and help from Sir John Summerson whom I have also consulted over various points of detail. Other friends who have been kind enough to provide advice and suggestions include Christopher Monkhouse, whose knowledge of London hotels is unrivalled, Nicholas Hallbritter and Anne Riches of the G.L.C. Historic Buildings Division. Dr Donald Olsen read the manuscript and made some extremely valuable suggestions. I would add that any errors are my sole responsibility.

Finally, I must pay tribute to James de la Mare for his enterprise and perseverance as picture researcher, to my photographer Godfrey New of Flemings, to Pete Pengilley the book designer, to Mrs Street for her cheerfulness, patience and efficiency in typing the manuscript, and to Rosalie Vicars-Harris of Queen Anne Press for her helpful criticism and editorial support.

# Contents

George IV, in 1822, by Sir Thomas Lawrence.

# Foreword

The city of London has been growing for the last 2000 years, but it is interesting to note that although the buildings in the centre have been replaced and modernised many times, the streets themselves have retained their locations, and in some cases they physically record the original planning decisions of Roman colonisers. The streets familiar to medieval Londoners still exist today, in spite of attempts to modernise after the Fire of 1666 and the Blitz of 1940, but the routes that for centuries had led Londoners out into the countryside are now no longer tracks but great thoroughfares.

London has grown bit by bit without any unifying plan and in direct response to the commercial pressures of the system of supply and demand. When buildings ceased to be viable they were replaced by new ones, but the street plan was hardly ever altered. It was not likely to be altered because the individual parishes were the only bodies responsible for improving the roads and streets and they could not afford anything but schemes of the smallest scale. London, therefore, was a collection of small streets and small houses arranged haphazardly in areas often dominated by a church.

The greater affluence of the eighteenth century caused London to expand at its West End. Here the countryside was owned by noble families who were in the fortunate position of being able to develop enough acres to create not only whole streets, but squares and whole communities at the same time. The use of architectural and town planning principles not only enriched the capital of a country that was now a world power, but also enriched the pockets of the landowners.

Adjacent to these fine new estates was a stretch of property that belonged to the Crown. It was an area more typical of scruffy, decaying Soho than of the new London, and when the leases reverted to the Crown, King George IV resolved to emulate the success of the new estates by redevelopment of this property, using the grandest architecture available.

Never before had any part of London been redeveloped with such thoroughness as this area of Regent Street, and, as it happened, London was never to have such another scheme. At only one moment of London's history was it considered appropriate for so large an area to be pulled down and replaced by 'Architecture with a capital A'.

Although the scheme was a success both commercially and architecturally this does not alter the fact that this kind of exercise was never repeated. London, unlike other European cities, was too democratic for redevelopment of this kind and it reverted to the usual pattern of gradual replacement of individual buildings.

This book explains the reasons for the building of Regent Street. It gives an account of all the different problems and how they were overcome. It goes on to show how its commercial success outpaced its success as a piece of urban design and how the inevitable modernisation of the shops transformed it into the street we know today.

It is interesting to note that although we now regard Regent's Park as the great monument to both Nash and the Prince Regent, the famous terraces were themselves threatened with demolition as recently as 1944. Therefore we should perhaps be grateful that there is still so much left to see of London's most successful attempts at classical town planning.

Richard Gloucester.

# Introduction

Regent Street is unique amongst London streets for several reasons. Many writers have seized on one or another of these, and a very great deal has been written about it in the century and an half of its existence. Few authors, whether Londoners or foreigners, have found it possible to ignore Regent Street—it has featured in guidebooks, history books, novels, reminiscences puerile and serious, in architectural journals and newspaper articles.

But people have not only written about Regent Street—they have gone there, and enjoyed going there for 150 years.

'Between three and six o'clock every afternoon, celebrities jostle you at every step you take in Regent Street. The celebrities of wealth, nobility and the mode, do not disdain to descend from their carriages, and tread the flags like ordinary mortals,' wrote George Augustus Sala in 1859.

Others came to see as well as be seen: 'Regent-street is not a business street, but a shopping centre. It is a broad leisurely thoroughfare, where every afternoon thousands of people stroll from window to window looking at the endless profusion of pretty things there displayed. Regent Street, in fact, to the millions who have passed along it consists of a ground floor and nothing else, with expensive or charming objects displayed attractively behind the wide plate-glass windows,' declared the *Standard* in 1912.

What is it that has attracted people to Regent Street for over a century? Why a book about Regent Street by itself rather than about the West End generally? What gives Regent Street its identity, an identity so strong that it has more in common with the rest of the long street than with the district through which it passes? What has enabled it to survive for a century and a half?

First of all, for over a century it has been, in Max Beerbohm's words, 'a happy hunting ground for the ardent shopper'. Shopping streets are perhaps what man creates towns for and Regent Street has long been a sumptuous market place. 'It stands unique the very soul centre of frivolous shopping where you buy most of the things you want and all the things that really you do not want, but which seem indispensable in a raid on London's shopping. You may get rid of money there with more irresponsibility and levity and laughter than anywhere else in London that I know.'

Alone amongst London's premier shopping streets, Regent Street was conceived as a 'bespoke' shopping avenue, created with royal support to fill a number of gaps in London's planning. It was designed to lead from a palace to a royal park, to open an important new residential area in Marylebone, and to provide a convenient route for the inhabitants of the West End to get to the Houses of Parliament, the Law Courts and the social life of St James's. It was intended to be not only a thoroughfare, it was to be a promenade for shoppers, to rival the newly created Rue de Rivoli, in Paris.

The Prince Regent, later King George IV, after whom it was named, saw it as an achievement which would 'quite eclipse Napoleon'; for this and other reasons he gave it his enthusiastic support, so his connection with Regent Street is very real. 'Of all the streets that have been named after famous men, I know but one whose namesake is

Regent Street in 1828 looking south from Oxford Circus. On the left is the Harmonic Institution as rebuilt by Nash in 1818, on the right the portico of the Hanover Chapel.

suggested by it. In Regent Street you sometimes think of the Regent; and that is not because the street is named after him, but because it was conceived by him, and was designed and built under his auspices, and is redolent of his character and his times.'

Max Beerbohm, who wrote that, is wrong in one thing—the 'New Street' was not the Prince's idea—but this does not detract from the credit due to him for his royal enthusiasm, and for the support he gave to his chosen architect, John Nash.

This book is an attempt very briefly to trace the story of Regent Street, its creation, development and its rebuilding. I have tried to give a picture of the people who have lived there, kept shops there, and who have visited it over the 150 years of its existence. It has been sketched, photographed and described by both visitors and Londoners, and I have drawn on these sources in order to give an idea of how it has appeared at different times, and how it has succeeded in keeping its appeal for five generations of Londoners.

LAWES

# I

# Metropolitan Improvements

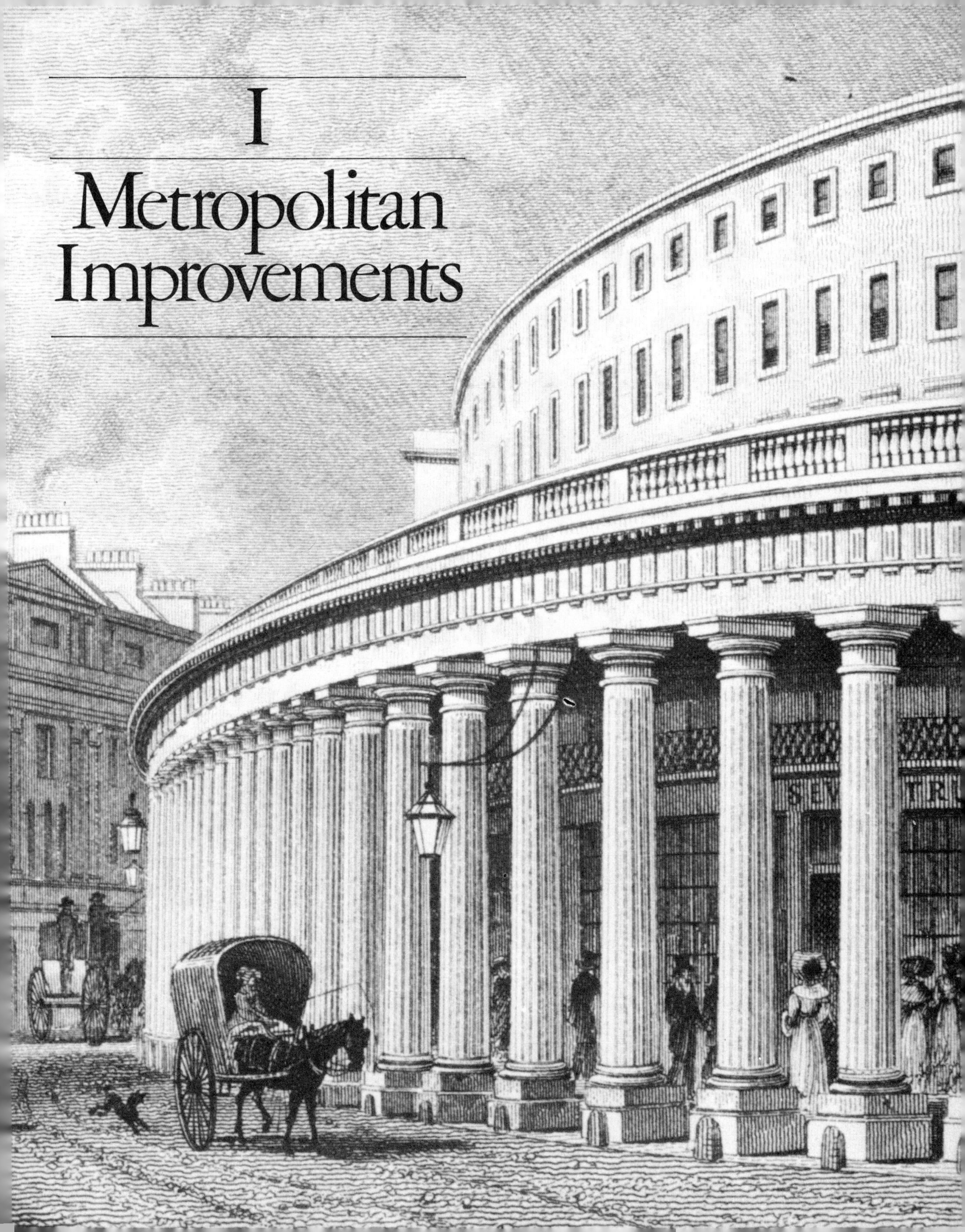

## Town planning schemes and opportunities in 1800

'AUGUSTUS made it one of his proudest boasts, that he found Rome of brick, and left it of marble. The reign and regency of GEORGE THE FOURTH have scarcely done less, for the vast and increasing Metropolis of the British empire: by increasing its magnificence and its comforts; by forming healthy streets and elegant buildings, instead of pestilential alleys and squalid hovels; by substituting rich and varied architecture and park-like scenery, for paltry cabins and monotonous cow-lairs; . . . and, by beginning and continuing with a truly national perseverance, a series of desirable improvements, that bid fair to render LONDON, the ROME of modern history.'

Thus wrote James Elmes in 1827 in a book called simply and arrogantly, *Metropolitan Improvements; or, London in the Nineteenth Century*. It is splendidly illustrated by one of the best and most comprehensive series of views of London ever published. Of the 170 or so drawings, over sixty are of 'improvements' in or connected with Regent Street and Regent's Park—the Regent's Canal at the north of the Park, Park Village on its eastern edge, and the new public open space between Charing Cross and the Strand which we know today as Trafalgar Square. For Regent Street must not be seen in isolation as a single road-widening and slum clearance scheme but as a radical reorganisation of an important central area, intimately and carefully linked to the rest of London's plan. It was designed to connect a large royal estate of some 500 acres, then known as Marybone Park, in the rural area north of Portland Place, with central London, with the additional benefit of improving the down-at-heel area round Pall Mall and the Haymarket, and easing the difficult traffic conditions round Charing Cross and the western end of the Strand.

It was seen by contemporaries as the first in a series of 'improvements' which would enable London to rank with other European capital cities, and remove the somewhat provincial image which she had hitherto enjoyed. The rather bombastic magniloquence, and the constant references to Rome, stem from a feeling of inferiority towards other capital cities, certainly as far as public buildings and public monuments went. When the Prince Regent spoke in 1811 of the new project 'quite eclipsing Napoleon' he was expressing a national, not only a personal, ambition.

This feeling of civic inferiority was much assuaged by a series of splendid new achievements portrayed by Elmes. The Londoner could admire with him the score of new churches, the new clubhouses, literary institutions and headquarters for learned bodies, the new government buildings, the hospitals and almshouses, and the new commercial buildings like the Custom House or Covent Garden Market. Of all the achievements however, none is more minutely described than the New Street.

If we look behind contemporary 'puff', and legend, it is clear that the ideas which brought into being the great series of metropolitan improvements which led from Marybone Park to Charing Cross, have a remarkably long history. They were in fact, developed by a number of men, not all of whom have taken as much credit as John Nash, the name, after the Prince Regent himself, most intimately connected with the project. It was Nash who finally brought the street into being, but he was building on foundations laid by a number of far-sighted and imaginative predecessors and colleagues.

As is so often the case it was man who 'built little but who thought and wrote much' who first suggested the West End Improvements in print. John Gwynn, a self-educated architect and architectural writer, published his *London and Westminster Improved* in 1766, and in this book he forecast a number of later town planning schemes. He was very distressed by the lack of overall planning in the West End of London, where individual estates were carefully laid out with little or no concern for their 'correspondence' with the property of other landowners. 'Why so wretched a use,' he observed, 'has been made of so desirable an opportunity of displaying the taste and elegance in this part of the town is a question that very probably would puzzle the builders themselves to answer'.

His contemporary, Horace Walpole, the writer and architectural amateur, was quite appalled by the growth of London. 'Though London increases every day . . . ,' he wrote in 1791, 'I believe you will think the town cannot hold all its inhabitants, so prodigiously the population is augmented . . . There will soon be one street from London to Brentford,

—aye, and from London to every village within ten miles round . . .'

Gwynn saw that the only hope for coherent planning in the expanding West End was a series of coordinated schemes working within a general plan. In his book he forecast Trafalgar Square, and sited Regent Street on the line of the Haymarket. Doubtless he was optimistic in suggesting that London should stop at the New Road, the modern Euston and Marylebone Roads—but ever since Queen Elizabeth's day planners and administrators have been hoping that London would settle down within reasonable limits, and we are still being disappointed!

After the visionary came the administrator. He was a Scottish civil servant, John Fordyce, (1735–1809) who was appointed surveyor-general of the Department of Woods and Forests in 1793.

He took office at a moment of great opportunity for the Department, since the lease of a large part of the Crown lands in London, Marybone Park, was about to expire. This was a large undeveloped estate of some 500 acres, consisting of three farms, a number of cottages, and one or two manufactories mostly connected with the building industry—a wheelwright's shop, a sculptor's workshop, and an artificial stone manufactory. The Park was bounded on the south by the New Road, now Marylebone Road, formed in 1756 to provide a through route from Paddington to the City, bypassing the West End. Development had taken place south of the Park, and to the west, but in the Park itself a series of leases had been granted to agricultural tenants, which had prevented building.

However these leases would end in 1811, and then Fordyce intended to develop this valuable Crown property, on the same lines as the adjoining aristocratic landowners, the Dukes of Portland and Bedford, and Lord Southampton, had done so profitably. Soon after his appointment, Fordyce had an up-to-date survey of the Park made. He obtained authority to offer a prize of £1000 for a scheme for laying out the estate.

This competition does not appear to have been widely advertised, and the 'architects of eminence' to whom copies were circulated, did not care, in the words of a later report, 'to bestow their time, and risk their reputation, in competitions of this nature'.

**Previous page** The Quadrant, and part of Regent Street in 1828

**Below** Marybone Park before development in 1792

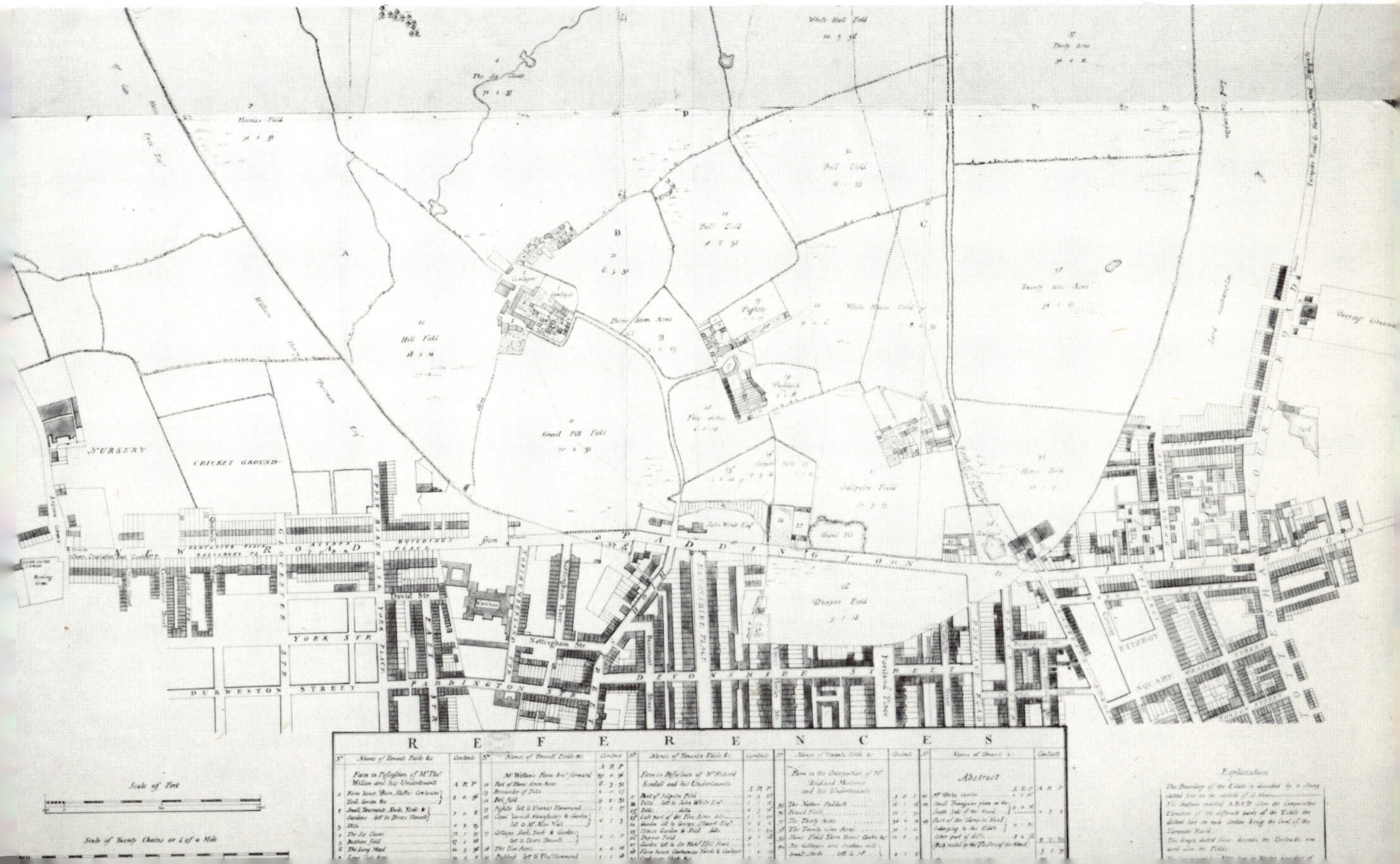

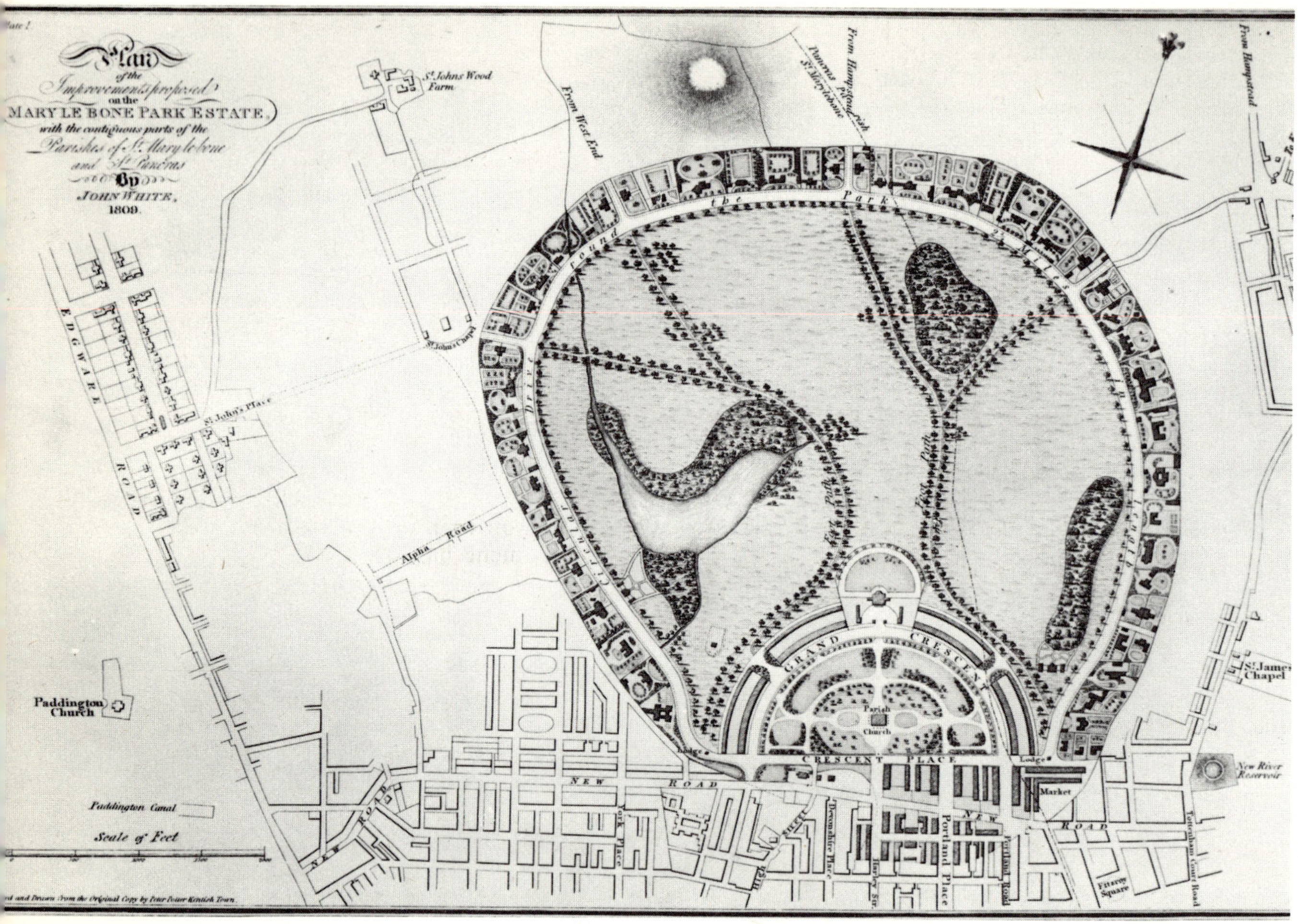


Only three plans were in fact submitted, all by John White, a resident in Marybone Park, who was surveyor to the Duke of Portland, one of the largest landowners in the parish. White's objects were set out by his son, who published his father's plans about 1813, anxious that 'it may be known that Mr White was the original proposer of a design so conducive to the health and comfort of the inhabitants of this part of the metropolis'. The principal object 'was that of forming an ornamental termination to this part of London, and of providing drives, rides and walks, which are very much wanted . . .' He also wished to protect the 'capital houses' already standing on the Portland estate from depreciation by haphazard and low development of the Park, or from dense development replacing the view of Highgate and Hampstead.

With these objectives he devised a ring of villas edging the park, with the centre open and laid out with a series of lakes and wooded walks. This was intended to serve the growing parish of Marylebone as the Royal Parks served the more favoured West End. White pointed out that wealthy villa owners would reduce the expense to the Crown by contributing to the costs of fencing and drainage, while the interior of the Park would continue like St James's Park, to provide grazing for cattle and sheep.

Meanwhile Fordyce was also concerned with a number of other town planning problems. These arose partly from the position of the Crown, represented by the Commissioners of Woods and Forests, as landlord in the Haymarket and elsewhere in St James's, and partly because of the role of the Commissioners in the absence of any metropolitan authority, as the coordinator of town planning schemes in London.

The Haymarket was dominated by the King's Theatre, or Opera House, one of the two most important theatres in London. After a disastrous fire it had been recently rebuilt to the designs of Michael Novosielski, but it still lacked a worthy facade to the Haymarket (see Plate II). At the south end of the Haymarket ran Pall Mall, then a very cramped and mean street. A proposal was put forward to widen Pall Mall at the east end, and to re-case the Opera House in colonnades on the east and south fronts with a 'Corridor of General Communication'—the forerunner of the Royal Arcade—on the west. These designs were prepared by Thomas Leverton, one of the Crown surveyors, in 1795–6. At the same period, proposals were put forward for the extension of Charles Street eastward to the Haymarket to improve the access to the King's Theatre in the Haymarket, and for the improvement of Market Lane, the narrow road which connected Pall Mall and Jermyn Street. The Charles Street proposal was incorporated in an Act of 1799, obtained by the would-be developer William Taylor, but on his failure to carry his scheme out within two years the right to do so reverted to the Crown.

In anticipation of improvement detailed surveys of the area were made by Thomas Chawner, from 1794–6, but owing to confusion about the ownership of the Opera House, and Fordyce's anticipation of the Marybone Park redevelopment no further action was taken.

At the east end of Piccadilly, the awkward turn into Tichborne Street and the bend into Marylebone Street were also inconvenient and here again a road-widening scheme was prepared by Chawner in 1796. One can see the beginnings of the Circus in the description: 'Those old Buildings (running out to a point) are to be pulled down, and one substantial brick Messuage [house] erected on a part of the ground, so as to leave a frontage of about 31 feet in Piccadilly, and the end or front towards Coventry-street to be set back, and finished with an elliptic Bow . . .'

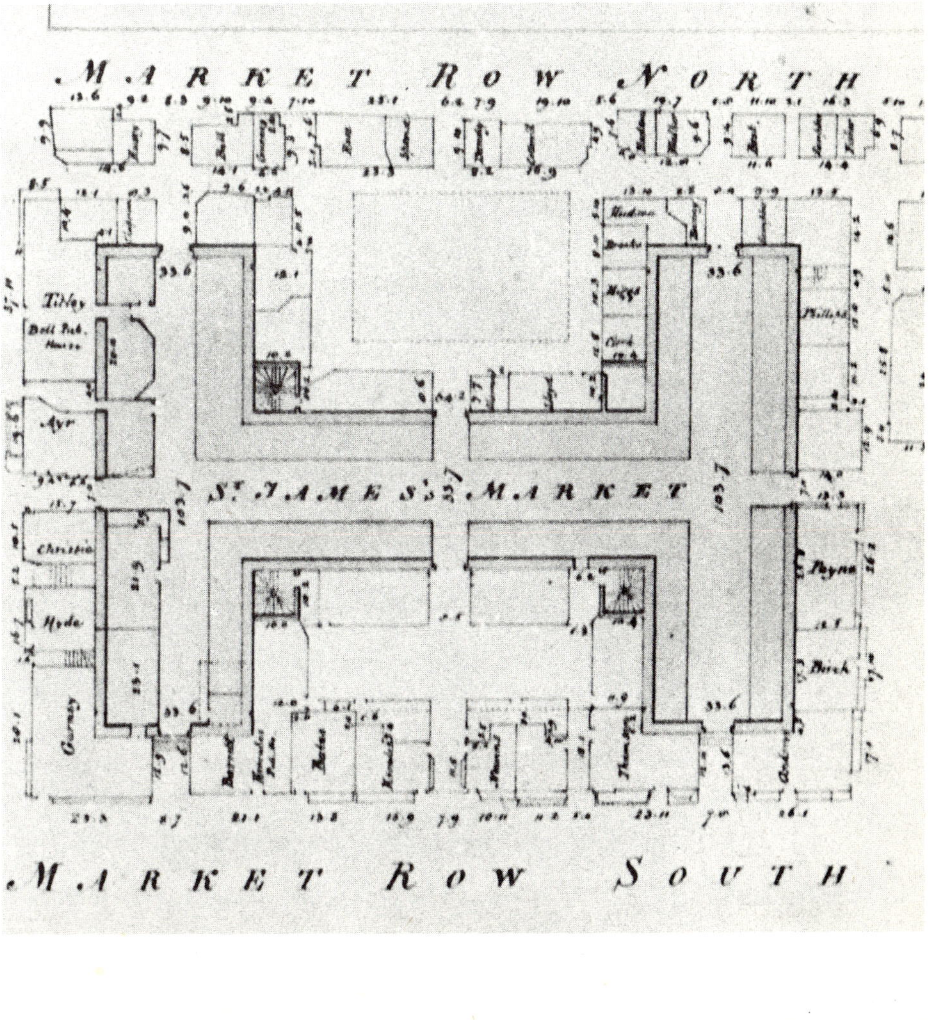


**Left** John White's Plan for Regent's Park, published by his son in 1813.
**Right** St James's Market from a survey made by Thomas Chawner in 1794.

With Crown property ripe for development north and south of Swallow Street, it was logical to see the need for a great north-south artery as an important public necessity. 'The distance and mean access, from Marybone Park to the Two Houses of Parliament, to Westminster Hall (which then housed the Law Courts), and to the several Public Offices in and near Whitehall, have always been considered as great drawbacks on the value of that ground for building.' Again Fordyce produced a solution—'a broad street in a direct line from about Charing-cross to the middle of the Southern Boundary of Estate', a scheme which made use of the dilapidated Royal Mews at Charing Cross for the southern part, and for which alternative routes were suggested either through Coventry Street to Piccadilly, and thence to Oxford Street or via Cockspur Street to Piccadilly, and thence northward. Leverton and Chawner indeed surveyed such a route in 1808 from the north of the Haymarket, 'nearly in the course of Great Windmill-street, communicating with Oxford-street, a little to the Eastward to the Pantheon', estimating the purchase of the Ground and Buildings at £290,000, and the sale of the old Materials and the surplus ground for building at £236,000 leaving a net cost of about £54,000, 'to accomplish this very desirable object, not only for the public convenience, but also for improving the value of that very extensive Estate, called Marybone Park . . .'

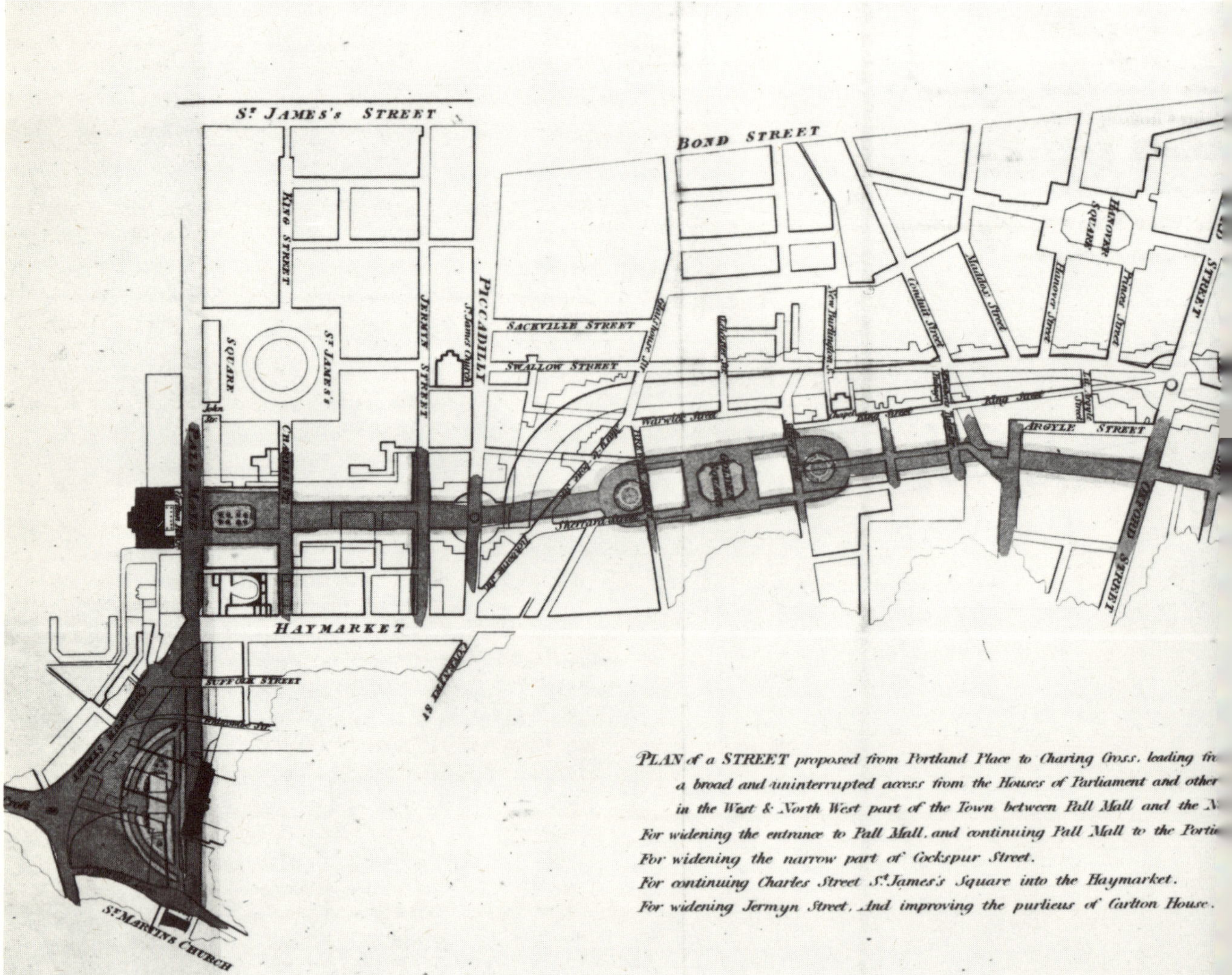

Most of the planning of the West End improvements can be seen to have been done by Fordyce—he had perceived the need for a new street, ordered the extensive surveys, and written the planners' brief for both Park and Street. Before the leases of the Park farms expired, and, perhaps more important, before the military tide had turned in the long Napoleonic wars, he died. His death in July 1809 was followed by yet another reorganisation at the Office of Woods and Forests. This time it was to be run by three Commissioners, with two secretaries, two surveyors and two architects working in the Office.

The two surveyors were Thomas Leverton, already one of the Crown surveyors, and his pupil, Thomas Chawner (1774–1851), who had already been working in the office, in a junior capacity. The two architects were John Nash and James Morgan, who had both been appointed by Fordyce himself in 1806. James Morgan appears to have been working for Nash in his private practice at the time when he was appointed Nash's deputy in his official post, so we may assume that he was in fact a Nash appointee.

John Nash's own appointment is a slightly more mysterious matter. A perfectly respectable reason for his employment was given in 1828, by Charles Arbuthnot, a member of the Select Committee investigating the Office of Works. Arbuthnot told the Committee that Nash had been appointed after he had caught the eye of Lord Robert Spencer, the First Commissioner of Woods and Forests at that time, by his competence in dealing with a bridge whose design had been mishandled by another architect. This seems quite plausible, and could well have been true, though more highly coloured versions were current at the time.

On the whole, however, no-one was concerned to suggest improprieties or mysteries in 1809, when Nash was appointed. Indeed, as the new scheme unfolded before Londoners, he became a hero, particularly in 1818, when Crabb Robinson could suggest that Regent's Park and the new street would give 'a sort of glory to the Regent's government, which will be more felt by remote posterity than the victories of Trafalgar and Waterloo, glorious as these are . . .' Unhappily, within ten years of these flattering words, Nash and his royal master had become the villains of the architectural scene—Nash perhaps qualifying for the unflattering distinction of being the most lampooned architect in British history.

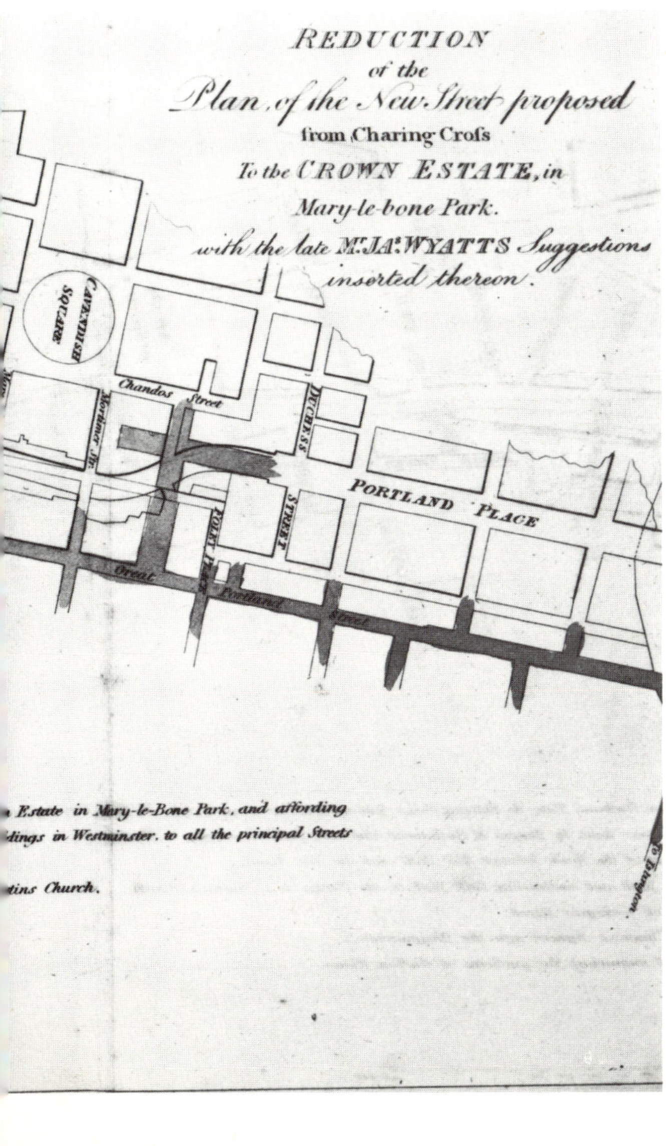


The new street from Charing Cross to the Crown Estate at Marybone Park. This map was published by John White junior in 1815, in his book on West End Improvements. He contrasts Nash's suggested line, as published in 1812, with a line to the east incorporating Golden Square, and crossing Oxford Street opposite Great Portland Street, which he attributes to James Wyatt (1746–1813). This line lies between that proposed by Nash, and that put forward by Leverton and Chawner in 1808.

# John Nash

J. Nash was appointed to the post of Architect to the Department of Woods and Forests in 1809, when he was 57 years old. It might be said that he had already had two architectural careers and was starting on a third.

He had trained in Robert Taylor's office, working his way up from a humble position. After working for Taylor for about ten years he had left to branch out on his own, not as an architect but as speculative builder and developer.

In 1783, after five years as a builder on his own, he went bankrupt, coming to grief over the doing up of three houses on the corner of Bloomsbury Square. The world of London development was closed to him—even after he was discharged it was impossible for him to get the credit on which any building business depended.

He moved to Wales, where he built up an architectural practice of a respectable and indeed, substantial character, starting with the design of Carmarthen Gaol in 1789, and graduating first to country houses in Wales and the Welsh marches, and to country house design throughout England and Wales. He built a number of country houses, many of which have been altered, and some demolished.

In 1796, he went into partnership with Humphrey Repton, one of the leading landscape architects of the day. Two years later the partners were working for the Prince of Wales at the Brighton Pavilion, where Nash is said to 'have attracted the favourable notice of the Prince Regent' for his work. Repton did the garden design side of the work, and Nash provided the architecture, a division of responsibility which proved satisfactory. It is not clear how much Nash did at Brighton on his own at this time—it seems more likely that he was designing architectural schemes like the conservatory exhibited at the Royal Academy in 1798, to fit in with Repton's landscape. As Sir John Summerson, Nash's biographer, points out, Repton carried out a good deal of work for the Prince at Brighton between 1797 and 1802, and Nash worked extensively for Repton during these years.

Nash's connection with the Prince Regent has always been mysterious and seems likely to remain so. The Prince of Wales was not Regent until 1811, and in 1798 he was still nursing the usual grievances and problems of any Crown Prince, dividing his time between dabbling in politics, the pursuit of ladies of the Carlton House set, and an increasing interest in the development and architectural adornment of his palaces. The formal residence of the sovereign at this period was St James's Palace, but there was inadequate accommodation for the entire family. In 1782 therefore, Buckingham House on the west side of St James's Park, had been bought for Queen Charlotte, while in 1783 the Prince of Wales had established himself at Carlton House. This was a much extended residence, which had been the centre of anti-government intrigue when it was the residence of the Prince's grandparents. The Prince's alterations to Carlton House established an unhappy pattern which became only too familiar. He overspent the money granted by Parliament, obtained more with promises of reform, and more again by agreeing to marry the Princess Caroline of Brunswick in 1795. Henry Holland was the first architect employed, and was responsible for the famous screened front facing Pall Mall, later intended as the terminus to the new street.

By 1786, however, the Prince was already turning his attention to the newly developed seaside resort of Brighton, where he was engaged on the building of a marine residence of an increasingly fantastic character. Like all his building projects, work began modestly, in 1786, under the direction of Henry Holland. Nash's first contribution came in 1798, and then only as the colleague of Repton.

However, Nash became more than the Prince's architect, he became a member of the Carlton House set. In 1806, partly because of the Prince's favour, and possibly because of the approval of Lord Robert Spencer (as suggested by Charles Arbuthnot), he obtained an official post in the Department of Woods and Forests. This, it is often suggested, had as much to do with the charms of Nash's young wife, Mary Anne Bradley, as with his not inconsiderable reputation as a country house architect.

The facts about Nash's marriage are curious, though as Sir John Summerson has concluded, the explanation of them is unlikely ever to emerge. In 1798, at the age of 46, he married Mary Anne Bradley, then 25, the attractive daughter of a West-

**Above** Carlton House and Pall Mall, in 1822.
**Left** John Nash, in 1827, from a portrait by Sir Thomas Lawrence.

minster coal merchant. Reputedly she was the mistress of the Prince Regent, a role which was the subject of a cartoon as late as 1820. The story is rendered more mysterious by the arrival on the scene of five Pennethorne children, born between 1798 and 1808, who are always described as distant maternal relations of Mrs Nash. Like Mrs Nash, the young Pennethornes were provided for by someone other than Nash, Nash leaving his money to his business associate John Edwards. James Pennethorne received an architect's training in Nash's office, succeeding his patron in due course as an official architect, becoming indeed the most influential government architect of the 1840s and 1850s.

The Nashes received a number of marks of princely favour. The Prince, when George IV, visited

Nash's house and office in Lower Regent Street, and a number of royal presents, from inlaid chairs to pearls and rings found their way to Mrs Nash. Certainly Nash was generally acknowledged to be the Prince's architect. When the post of Surveyor-General fell vacant on the death of James Wyatt, Lord Liverpool wrote that the 'Prince Regent is naturally desirous of employing his own architect Mr Nash . . .' Perhaps for this reason it was decided to split the post up, and employ three men, all working on a part time basis, instead of one. The other two were John Soane (1753–1837) and Robert Smirke (1781–1867), and though they shared out the official work, Nash's position as the royal favourite obtained for him the work which involved most dealings with the Prince. Thus in 1821, when the decision was taken to refurbish Buckingham Palace for George IV, who had succeeded the previous year, and wanted a new royal palace, Nash was given the job. This was not strictly according to the etiquette for dividing up the official work. In a letter about the incident to Sir John Soane who was entitled to expect the job, Nash expressed the relationship between the three men, and also underlined his own security as the royal favourite:

'Brother Soane,

You was in a miff when I saw you at the head of your Masons. One of the Masonic rules, I am told, is to acquire a meek and humble spirit. I fear therefore that you are not qualified for Grand Master . . . When I left You . . .—it occurred to me that our appointments are perfectly constitutional, I, the King, You, the Lords, and *Your* friend Smirke, the Commons, and the blood instantly rushed to my face seeing, or fancying that You wanted to dethrone me . . .'

However, in 1809, when Nash was appointed to the post of Architect to the Woods and Forests, all this fame and much of the royal favour lay in the future. This was his golden opportunity, and century old gossip about how exactly he obtained it is not perhaps important or relevant to the story of Regent Street. What is important, however, is that for reasons personal or professional, Nash caught the eye of the Prince of Wales on the eve of his appointment as Regent, and was launched on a new career as an official architect. The rich town planning opportunities envisaged by White, planned by Fordyce and surveyed by Chawner, fell into his capable hands. His unsuccessful period as a London speculative builder which ended in bankruptcy, and his work as a romantic country house architect, provided the training to turn the utilitarian route from Marybone Park to Westminster through the slums of Soho into the elegant commercial thoroughfare of Regent Street.

Cartoon of George IV and Mrs Nash published in 1820, aboard the royal yacht near Cowes.

# The West End of London in 1811

The West End of London in 1800 was a patchwork of different interests, developed over the previous century to different standards, depending on ownership and size of estate. To the west side of the proposed line of the new street lay prosperous streets and squares, to the east older, smaller houses, some originally fashionable but now let out as lodgings.

South of Marybone Park interposed the enormous Cavendish-Harley estate, originally laid out to the design of John Prince in 1719, and recently extended by the brothers Adam into Portland Place. It was basically a scheme of squares and streets—the occasional large square gave *cachet* and a good address to the surrounding streets, which were carefully graded as to size of house. Thus Cavendish Square served the streets north of Oxford Street, while Hanover Square, laid out slightly earlier by Lord Scarborough, served those to the south. In both cases the landowners and the developers who had taken the land were concerned with creating a prosperous and attractive residential area, and shops and tradesmen generally were banished to back streets. The Cavendish-Harley estate did build a market, the Oxford Market, to serve the estate, but it was carefully tucked away on the less fashionable east to avoid 'damaging' the estate.

Further south Swallow Street formed, in Nash's words, 'the Line of Separation between the habitations of the first classes of society, and those of the inferior classes'. On the west lay Savile Row and Burlington Street, laid out in the second and third decades of the eighteenth century by the great amateur architect Lord Burlington. To the east, a number of smaller landowners had developed land originally belonging to the Crown in a variety of street patterns, whose plans still reflected field boundaries dating from Tudor times. A number of these properties were traded by the Crown in Stuart times for interests in property near St James's Park, but some had been retained, notably that between Swallow Street on the west, stretching eastward to Marlborough Row, southward to Beak Street, and northward to Foubert's Passage.

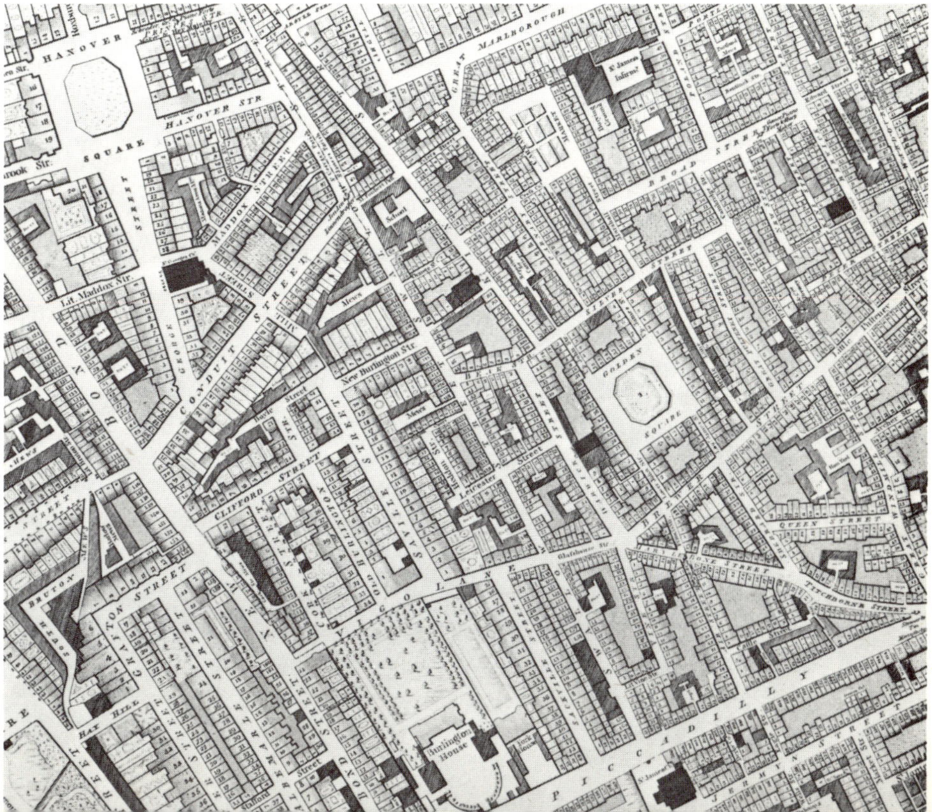


Map showing the Swallow Street area in 1792.

Immediately south of Oxford Street on the east side of Swallow Street, a small street, King Street (modern Kingly Street), which was originally the footpath from Piccadilly to St Marylebone, diverged from Swallow Street, running south-eastwards to the junction of Marylebone and Glasshouse Streets. On the east again lay the Argyll Estate, built up by the second Duke of Argyll, and laid out in the years following 1735 apparently to the design of R. Morris. The most important and fashionable street, Argyll Street, lay too far east to be in danger from the New Street, but a small connection with Swallow Street, called Little Argyll Street, had been opened, on the corner of which stood a well-known set of concert rooms, the Argyll Rooms.

Swallow Street ran in a straight but narrow course to the parish church of St James's in Piccadilly. Between Foubert's Passage and Beak Street, it provided the boundary for Crown property and that of the Burlington estate. Foubert's Passage commemorated one of the more colourful members of the *émigré* Huguenot community which had settled in Soho, and established a tradition of foreign occupation which has only recently been eroded. Much of this occupation took place further east where the fashionable Poland Street housed no less than three foreign legations in the mid-eighteenth century.

Major Henry Foubert established his riding and fencing school in the premises fronting on to Swallow Street at the beginning of the eighteenth century, and the establishment continued as a riding school until 1782. Then the long covered 'Ride' and the stables were let to a liveryman and the 'academy' to the parish as a training school for pauper children.

Between Beak Street and Vigo Street lay the Pulteney Estate, originally laid out about 1673 in a simple cruciform design divided by Swallow and Leicester Streets. In 1721 the Pulteney Estate bought the freehold of most of the area except for the south-western quarter which remained the property of the Crown, and was apparently covered by rather poor buildings, largely livery stables.

Swallow Street, which took its name from a sixteenth century tenant, Thomas Swallow, seems to have been a street regretted by few. One Victorian antiquarian described it as a 'long, ugly and irregular thoroughfare', and even the Victorian journalist George Sala, who found endless fascination in the Regent Street area, could only describe it as a 'long, devious, dirty thoroughfare called Great Swallow Street, which three generations since, was full of pawnbrokers, dramshops, and more than equivocal livery stables, which were said to be extensively patronised by professional highway men . . .'

South of Piccadilly, the property all belonged to the Crown, and again was in poor order. This seems to have been due partly to problems connected with the length of leases which the Crown was originally able to grant, and partly to the somewhat lackadaisical management of the Department of Woods and Forests which Fordyce had found in the management of Marybone Park. East of St James's Square, then one of the grandest addresses in London, lay several small streets, grouped round the St James's Market, laid out on the estate of Lord St Albans in 1663. In 1720 the market was renowned for the quality of its provisions, which were especially provided for 'the Stewards of People of Quality, who spare no Price to furnish their

Lords' Houses with what is nice and delicate'. By 1800 the market house was over a hundred years old and dilapidated. Even the Haymarket, where an important market in hay and straw still took place, and which was a major street connecting Piccadilly and Pall Mall, was lined on the east side with inn yards. This was partly due to the importance of Piccadilly as a terminus for long-distance mail coaches, particularly to the west of England. At No. 75, stood the Three Kings, with a galleried yard which survived into the mid-nineteenth century, famous as the terminus of the first Bath coach. Its equally famous rival, the White Horse Cellar, stood at the corner of Dover Street, and after the coach services had been superseded by the railway, continued as a terminus for one of the feeder horse bus services which ran between Paddington and London Bridge stations and the West End.

On the south side of Piccadilly stood the White Bear Inn, in the occupation of Isaac Clemmill. He also owned a coaching office next door, the White Bear's extensive stabling, and that of the Lemon Tree on the corner of the Haymarket, both yards with stabling for over forty horses. Further south, there were the Black Horse, the Cock, the George, the Bell, and finally a stable yard behind the Opera House, which was apparently part of the theatre complex.

**Left** Major Foubert's Stables and covered ride in Swallow Street.
**Right** Argyll House, Argyll Street, in 1854, built as the town mansion of the Duke of Argyll in 1750. It survived as a nobleman's mansion till 1862, being occupied from 1808 until 1860 by Lord Aberdeen, the diplomat and statesman. The Palladium stands on its site today.

The White Bear Inn in Piccadillly.

# II

# The creation of Regent Street

# Nash's Grand Design

In October 1810 the Department of Woods and Forests finally commissioned two schemes for the new street and for laying out the Park. One of these was from Leverton and Chawner, who had done so much of the ground work, and the other from Nash and Morgan. They also considered and gave a small prize to John White's scheme. It has been suggested that Leverton and Chawner were only employed as a check on Nash's financial forecasts, but, even if this was not so, in an age when royal favour was still the high road to official advancement, Nash could hardly have been preferred so blatantly to the two senior architects.

Leverton and Chawner referred the Commissioners to the survey they had made in 1808 for the line from the Haymarket to Oxford Street, but provided a new scheme for Marylebone Park itself. This was largely based on the traditional London scheme—the grand square with subsidiary squares and crescents linked by streets of varied degrees—very similar to the layout planned for the Bedford Estate on which Leverton had worked. The sole concession to the rural character of the site was the detached and semi-detached villas laid out in regular lines over the northern part of the Park and the irregular crescent devised to take advantage of the peninsular portion known as Dupper Field.

Nash's scheme was not only more imaginative and attractive, it was more 'comprehensive, yet generally speaking, rational and practicable' and the Commissioners had little hesitation in recommending its acceptance, in outline at least, to the Lords of the Treasury. They were the ultimate arbiters of what was, after all, a scheme for relieving the taxpayers' pockets by increasing the Crown revenues.

Nash's original plan for the Park involved the building of terraces only. He pushed the Life Guard Barracks away to the furthest corner of the Park and kept the formal groups of houses, both straight terraces and crescents, to the edge of the Park, except for a substantial double circus in the centre. He provided smaller houses on the eastern edge for tradesmen, and a large market area, doubtless intended to serve the growing Camden Town to the east as well as the substantial residents of the Park itself. This market, the barracks and also the Park when 'building' was to be served by a new canal, already projected, which was to connect the Grand Union Canal at Paddington with the Thames below London Bridge.

The 'London Canal' as it was originally known, had been the project of Thomas Homer, a promoter who had commissioned a survey from John Rennie as early as 1802. He had revived the project in 1810, approached John Nash, who had adopted the idea with enthusiasm, and had become involved in the actual promotion of the Canal in the early part of 1811, before his scheme had even been submitted to the Commissioners, let alone approved. The story of the building of the Canal, and of Nash's financial involvement, is long and complicated, and has more to do with Regent's Park than Regent Street. It was, however, this penchant of John Nash for becoming commercially involved in schemes where he was acting in a professional capacity which was such a useful handle for his enemies. Later, when he was being investigated by one parliamentary committee after another, many searching questions were asked about his involvement in the supply of bricks to Regent Street, his profits from speculation in sites in Suffolk Street, his role as a marble supplier for Buckingham Palace—all turned on this question of commercial involvement. Sir John Summerson has dealt very fully with Nash's fatal talent for becoming involved commercially, though perhaps not always very profitably, in his professional undertakings. Of course, it was then regarded as perfectly proper for architects to be involved in building speculation—it was the early Victorians who developed the modern distinction between architect and builder, but even in a more easy-going age, it was thought that Nash had overstepped the mark.

The route of the Canal through the Park, and indeed the layout of the Park itself, were later much modified. The Canal was pushed up to the northern rim, the Life Guards moved out of the smart residential area of the Park altogether. Nash retained his terraces round the edge of the Park but adapted Leverton's idea of villas for the centre, and also rejected the idea of a circus at the top of Portland Place. This was intended to solve the problem of crossing the New Road.

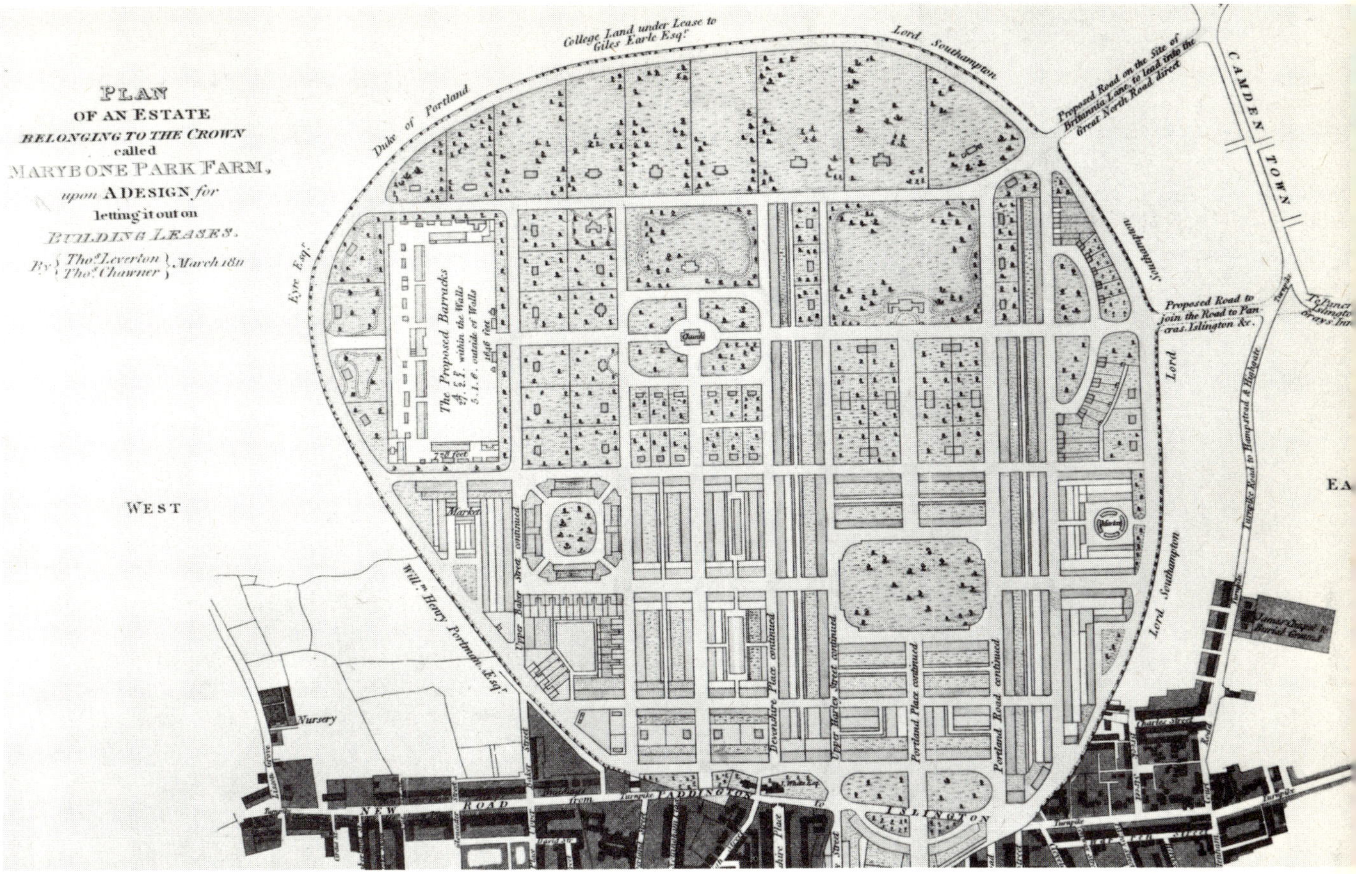


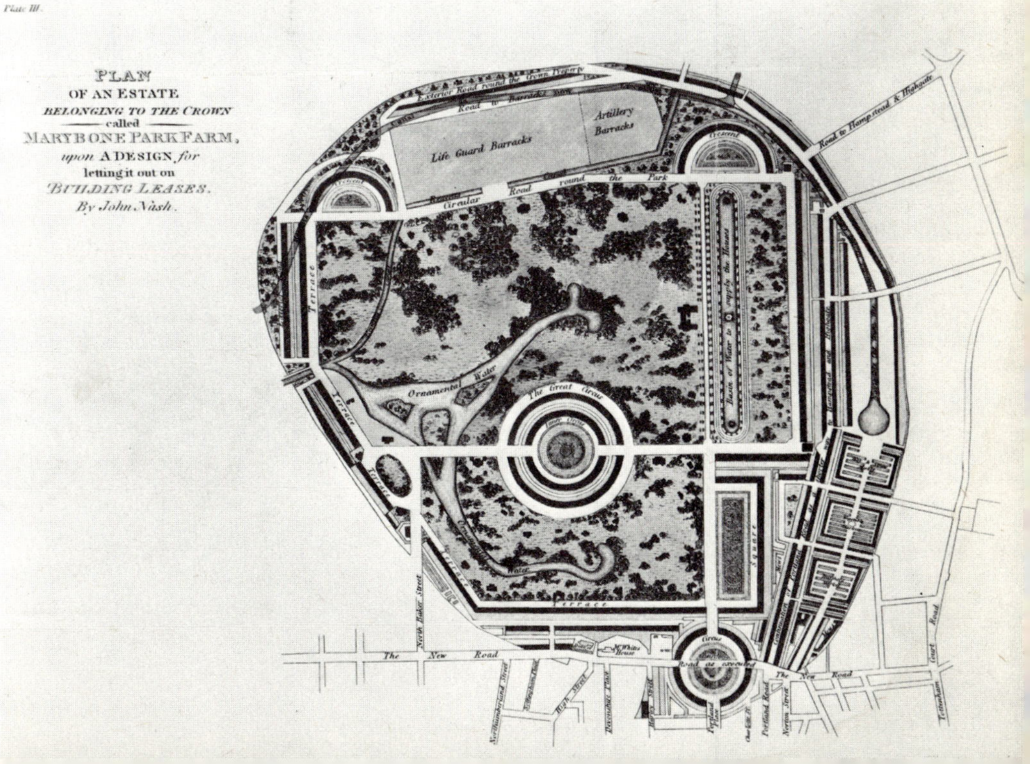


**Above** Leverton and Chawner's scheme for Regent's Park, 1811.
**Right** John Nash's Original Scheme for Regent's Park, 1811. The original route of the Canal has been amended in manuscript on this copy.

**Previous page** East side of Park Square and the Diorama, 1827

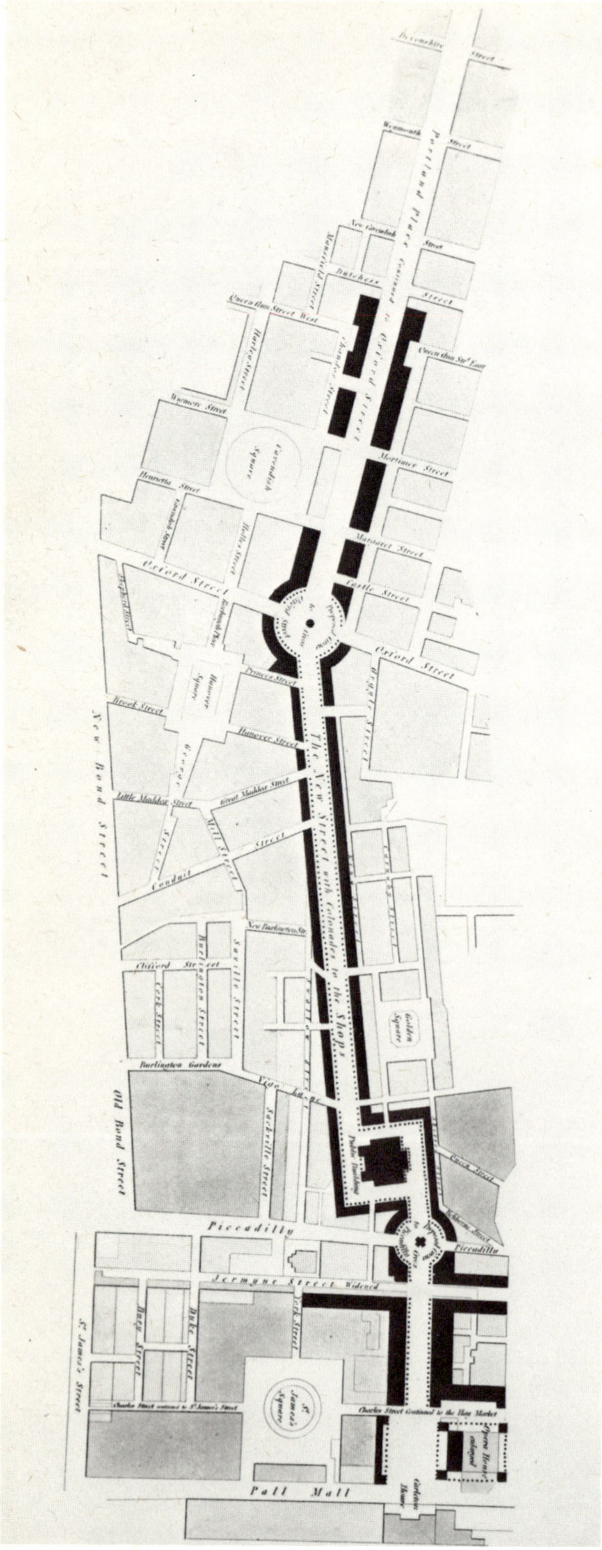

**Above** Waterloo Place and Carlton House in 1818.

**Left** Nash's Original Scheme for Regent Street, July 1811. This took a route considerably further west across the line of Piccadilly, to avoid Golden Square. Portland Place was extended southward to cut Oxford Street.

Portland Place, being the widest street in London, was taken by Nash as the model for the New Street. He wrote a lengthy and detailed report to support the line proposed for the New Street. Bond Street, he pointed out, was the 'most convenient, and therefore the street almost exclusively used as the access to the numerous spacious and elegant squares and streets north of Oxford Road . . . (and for that reason the shops appropriated to fashion have established themselves in Bond Street and its vicinity), insomuch that the throng of carriages, horses, and foot-passengers . . . choke up the passage . . .' To replace it on the line of Poland Street as suggested by Leverton and Chawner would mean that it would be separated from the fashionable West End by 'Air-Street, Swallow-Street, Warwick-Street, King-Street, and all the alleys, alehouses, and lanes between'.

Beginning therefore with Pall Mall, 'always one of the inlets to the West-end of the town', he suggested that the cramped eastern end should be widened to its fullest extent right through to the Haymarket. An island site would thus be provided for the Opera House, whose situation, (and that of the Haymarket Theatre) would be further improved by the extension eastwards of Charles Street into the Haymarket. No more openings eastward were to be provided between Charles Street and Piccadilly so 'that the footpath would be uninterrupted by Crossings; and the inferior houses, and the traffic of the Hay-market, would be cut off. . .'

The axis of Carlton House was too far east, and in order to move the street westward to cut Piccadilly half way between Air Street and the end of Titchborne Street, Nash proposed 'to form a small Circus where the oblique lines meet in

**Left** Foley House, Portland Place, in 1809. It was built in 1758 for Lord Foley, who obtained from the Duke of Portland an undertaking that his view northwards should not be interrupted by housing. It occupied the southern end of Portland Place, and stood in the way of the new street. It was bought by Nash personally, and immediately demolished.
**Right** Piccadilly from Coventry Street, in 1830. This print, made after the creation of Regent Street, demonstrates Nash's skill at crossing a street 'imperceptibly', and should be compared with the view of Piccadilly in 1909, page 76–77.

Piccadilly, and to place a Column, or other public Monument, in the centre; at the same time that the obliquity of the lines of the street is concealed, the situation will be most eligible for a public Monument, as it will interrupt the view, and arrest the attention of all who pass along those streets of general intercourse'. He placed considerable emphasis on the importance of this monument, both as 'a central object terminating the Vista' from Carlton House, as Carlton House did from Piccadilly, and as a beautiful object in its own right. It is probably not unfair to suggest that, had Nash's scheme been carried out unaltered, we might have had a statue dedicated to the Prince, rather than one of Eros dedicated to Lord Shaftesbury. In any case, in view of the sad later history of Piccadilly Circus, Nash's intentions are of particular interest.

The next major obstacle for circumnavigation lay between Piccadilly and Oxford Street:
'. . . it will be necessary to form a small square, in order to avoid Golden-square, the Area of which small Square will afford a Site for a Theatre, or any other public Building, to which its central situation will be particularly applicable; this Break in the straight Line will make the remaining Street less oblique, and avoid the necessity of purchasing any of the Houses which form Golden-square.'

Only the grandest streets on the west—New Burlington Street, Conduit Street, Hanover Street, and Princes Street—would open into the new street, the rest would be served by the rump of Swallow Street, while on the east Brewer Street, Silver [Beak] Street, Marlborough Street and Argyll Street would connect with it:
'thus . . . Carts and Drays can carry on their traffic by means of the back streets without interfering with the Principal Street.
. . . the whole Communication from Charing-Cross to Oxford-street will be a boundary and complete separation between the Streets and Squares occupied by the Nobility and Gentry, and the narrower Streets and meaner Houses occupied by mechanics and the trading part of the community.'

This was an earlier and more extended exposition of Nash's well-known nautical phrase about 'hugging all the avenues which went to good streets'.

North of Oxford Street, the line was given simplicity and grandeur by continuing Portland Place southwards into Oxford Street; Foley House, which then closed the southern end, being 'immediately pulled down'.

The crossing of Oxford Street presented almost the same problems as that of the New Road, and another Circus and public monument as that for the crossing of Piccadilly was proposed, so 'that the sensation of having passed Oxford-street will be entirely done away, and the two divisions of the

Town insensibly united in the best manner possible'.

The directness of the new street would, Nash was at pains to point out, bring 'Mary-le-bone Park . . . nearer to the Houses of Parliament, Courts of Law, and Public Offices, than four parts out of five of the principal residences in the West and North-west ends of the Town'.

It is revealing that Nash alone of the contributors to the voluminous report of the Commissioners transmutes the traditional and apparently generally accepted 'Marybone' into the more romantic and elegant 'Mary-le-bone'. This romantic and ambitious approach was the keynote of the original Nash plan: he was not content to develop the Park in the well-tried traditional West End pattern and then connect it via Oxford Street to the Haymarket. Fired by the commercial success of Bond Street he saw the central portion of the new street between the two circuses become 'the great thoroughfare' in which:

'. . . shops appropriated to articles of taste and fashion will . . . arrange themselves . . . and the stream of fashion be diverted to a new Street, where the Footpath will be 15 feet wide, instead of 7 feet, and the Carriage-way double the width of that in Bond-street, and where there will be room for all the fashionable shops to be assembled in one Street . . .'

Greater attraction and convenience would be given to this grand street, some 120 feet wide, by 'a light Colonnade, surmounted by a Balustrade' over the foot-pavements, projecting over both the shops on the ground floor and the mezzanine living-quarters of the shopkeepers. These would thus form an architectural and visual distinction between the shops themselves and the floors which were intended to be let as lodgings. The balconies would prove attractive as points of vantage for lodgers 'to converse with those passing in the Carriages underneath', but as the colonnades were also intended to protect the shoppers and others 'frequently confined many days together to their Houses by rain', possibly the colonnades were destined to be more useful than the balconies.

Drainage of the new street presented a considerable problem, though two major sewers ran down from Regent's Park into the Thames. One was the King's Scholars' Pond Sewer, which ran down from Regent's Park to Mayfair, then through St James's Park, and out to the Thames through Pimlico in a twenty-foot wide cut, used at its mouth as a timber dock. It already 'drained all the palaces in the West End' very inadequately, and it was not thought it could do any more. John Rennie had reported on the problem and dismissed it with the conclusion that 'a sewer that is to perform its work by constant attention to repairs, is not fit for the Metropolis of the British Empire'.

The Hartshorn Sewer running down the Soho

side of the new street was in no better state, and it was decided to create a new sewer down the centre of the new street which was to pick up some of the drains in Pall Mall, and discharge into the Thames near Charing Cross. This new sewer was a major charge on the Commissioners, costing some £50,000 to construct.

Most of the arguments and obstacles were explored in Nash's report of July 1811, but though the Commissioners commended his scheme to the Treasury, modifications were demanded and indeed forced on the Commissioners and their architect. Nash provided two alternative schemes for the central portion. One of these brought the new street across Piccadilly by St James's Church, and the other showed the curving street 'resembling in that respect the High Street at Oxford' which was finally adopted.

North of Oxford Street, Nash had second thoughts about taking his street through the valuable 'Yards and Gardens belonging to the Houses on the East side of Cavendish Square'—a line which he feared might prove expensive. In consequence, he suggested a sweep eastward and a line making use of Edward and Bolsover Streets. Both of these alterations were incorporated in the map attached to the New Street Act.

The Act appointed a Commission to organise the making and management of the new street, a favourite administrative device of the period. It also authorised the considerable amount of compulsory purchase of houses not already belonging to the Crown, laid down terms for compensation, and regulated the procedures to be followed. It also authorised the Commissioners to borrow money: a maximum of £600,000. The Bill was debated in Parliament in June 1813, and despite opposition from the shopkeepers of Bond Street, who had legitimate worries about competition, and concern from other quarters about the expense of the new street, the Bill was passed in July 1813.

Regent's Park and Regent Street, despite the 1813 Act and the involvement of the Crown, were developed like any contemporary private speculation, whether on one of the grand ducal estates or in a suburban field in south London. Nash's role was that of a contemporary estate surveyor, and the builders and developers with whom he dealt were often men already engaged on similar developments elsewhere in London.

The system was one which had emerged in the seventeenth century and had been gradually refined and sophisticated as more and more Londoners put

**Above** Carlton House from Waterloo Place showing the royal palace on the axis of the new street as intended by Nash.
**Left** 'A Toad under a Harrow', June 20 1829. A cartoon published after the Select Committee on Crown Leases had examined Nash's behaviour. 'Suffolk Street Job' and 'Artists' Gallery Job' both refer to Nash's taking of leases in Suffolk Street, 'Marble Job' and 'Pimlico Job' refer to Buckingham Palace, and the half-hidden 'Brick . . .' to his brickmaking activities in Regent's Park.

their savings or their little bit of capital into a house here, a terrace there, or into some ground rents. A landlord or head lessee with ground 'ripe for development' would make a building agreement for a number of plots with a developer, either a builder who would undertake the actual erection of the houses, or with a solicitor or banker, who would employ a builder to erect houses, or would sublet in his turn. The chain often developed a large number of links, it being understood that a man of substance who took on a large block, perhaps laying out the roads, and making the basement vaults, was entitled to a higher profit than a small man who might engage only for a single site. The lease was granted on the completion of the building, either to the actual builder or to his nominee.

The skill and expertise of the estate surveyor, aided by the owner of the estate and his solicitor or estate manager, were required to gauge exactly how hard a bargain to drive with would-be developers. It was well understood that unreliable men might offer a better deal but be unable to complete their 'take', and for this reason competitive tenders were not employed in the making of Regent Street.

The Commissioners of Woods and Forests, operating from the New Street Office, behaved as the Grosvenor Board or the Bedford Estate Office would have behaved in managing a similar development. It seems likely, however, that Nash, being responsible directly to the Commissioners, at that time a group of M.P.'s and other public men, with not very senior civil service clerks working in the office, was left more independence than he would have been on a private estate. This meant that he was a great deal more involved in the difficult land agent's side of the letting, as well as in the 'surveyor's' role of preparing designs, supervising construction, and drawing up lease plans. Sir John Summerson has suggested that Nash's architecture suffered from a lack of concentration in the designing stage, and that 'it suffered even more (as he admitted himself) from being carried out by builders without the architect's direct supervision'.

Taken all in all, however, the depth of Nash's involvement in the street, in such a number of roles—as architect, surveyor, estate agent, even developer, lessee and resident—merely confirms his right to much of the credit. In a manner typical of many important developers, he put together a motley team of lesser developers, builders, solicitors and amateurs, who had had 'a great deal to do in the purchase of ground-rents', and 'were in the habit of advancing money to builders', and cajoled and encouraged them, bullied and threatened them, to complete first one engagement and then another. He set an example by building a magnificent house on an important site himself, and when another site was sticking, made an offer 'with all the warmth of heart and in the liberal way in which he does everything'.

It seems possible that Nash had hoped for a more organised system of development since, in his original report to the Commissioners, he indulged in a swingeing attack on the worst aspects of the traditional London system of development. It is worth quoting because it shows what Nash had to contend with in his role of surveyor:

'The artificial causes of the extension of the Town are the speculations of Builders, encouraged and promoted by Merchants dealing in the materials of Building, and Attornies with monied Clients facilitating, and indeed putting in motion, the whole system, by disposing of their Client's Money in premature Mortgages, the sale of improved Ground-Rents, and by numerous other devices, by which their Clients make an advantageous use of their Money, and the Attornies create to themselves a lucrative business from the Agreements, Assignments, Leases, Mortgages, Bonds, and other instruments of Law, which become necessary. . . .'

Nash found an Insurance Company, the Royal Exchange, who were prepared to advance a direct loan of £300,000 for immediate expenses such as the purchase of houses or the making of sewers and roadways, but this was not enough and a further advance of working capital was made, reluctantly, by the Bank of England in December 1816. The limit set by the Act for loans to the New Street Commissioners was £600,000, and even with this size of loan, the development of the new street was heavily dependent on private capital, from both speculating builders and 'attornies with monied clients'. After this attack, Nash's difficulties in finding takers and developers may well have caused a certain amount of pleasure east of Lincoln's Inn Fields.

In fact, John Nash had a very wide responsibility, nominally under the supervision of the Office of Woods and Forests, for all aspects of the creation of Regent Street. He was responsible for measuring and valuing any ground or buildings to be purchased for the new street, as a leasehold interest either from the Commissioners' own Crown tenants, or from outside landowners and tenants. He was to prepare all designs for new buildings, to set out the ground and to negotiate with prospective tenants both over terms and the types and designs of buildings to be erected. He also performed the usual estate surveyor's duty of certifying new buildings for the granting of leases, and of providing plans to be inserted in the margin of the lease. In addition he undertook the supervision of the buildings during erection to make sure that the materials and workmanship were up to the agreed standard. In return for this he received a percentage on the rents and on the proceeds of the sales of old materials, usually sold to the developer who had taken that part of the ground and paid for at 20 years' purchase—that is five per cent of their value was added to the ground rent. These old materials were a significant figure—one estimate by Leverton and Chawner, characteristically more modest than that of Nash, put the total value of old materials in the new street at £129,748, about ten per cent of the total value of the property affected. Regency builders had little to learn about re-cycling—old bricks and even timber from other industries like ship-building found their way into houses at a time of boom.

Nash himself thought that he was 'remunerated very badly' for his design work, since the Commissioners drove a hard bargain with him over the exact terms, when they finally got down to signing an agreement. This did not happen until 1815, and even then there had to be a 'subsequent explanatory statement', 'without which the original agreement was of very little use'. Up until 1814 Nash was paid a lump sum of £1000 with a further lump sum of £2,500 for all the complex and detailed work connected with the important new sewer from the Park to Charing Cross. For unremunerative and non-commercial work like public open spaces, public buildings and so forth, Nash received five per cent on the value of the work, a fairly usual architect's percentage at the time, while on the immediately assessable letting of plots of land he received a half-year's rent (the full term was usually 99 years) and one quarter per cent on valuations.

Nash did not confine himself to the role of an architect and surveyor where the new street was concerned. There is evidence that he speculated in sites both in Regent's Park near the Commercial Basin, and in Suffolk Street at the bottom of the Haymarket.

**Right** The King's Theatre, Haymarket, as rebuilt to the design of Michael Novosielski in 1790. Behind this façade was a large concert room in which Haydn gave a famous series of concerts in 1795. The well-known colonnaded façade by Nash and G. S. Repton was added between 1816 and 1818. *Plate II*

**Below** The Little Theatre in the Haymarket, pulled down in 1820, for the building of the Theatre Royal, Haymarket. It was built in 1720, on a site to the north of the present Haymarket Theatre. *Plate I*

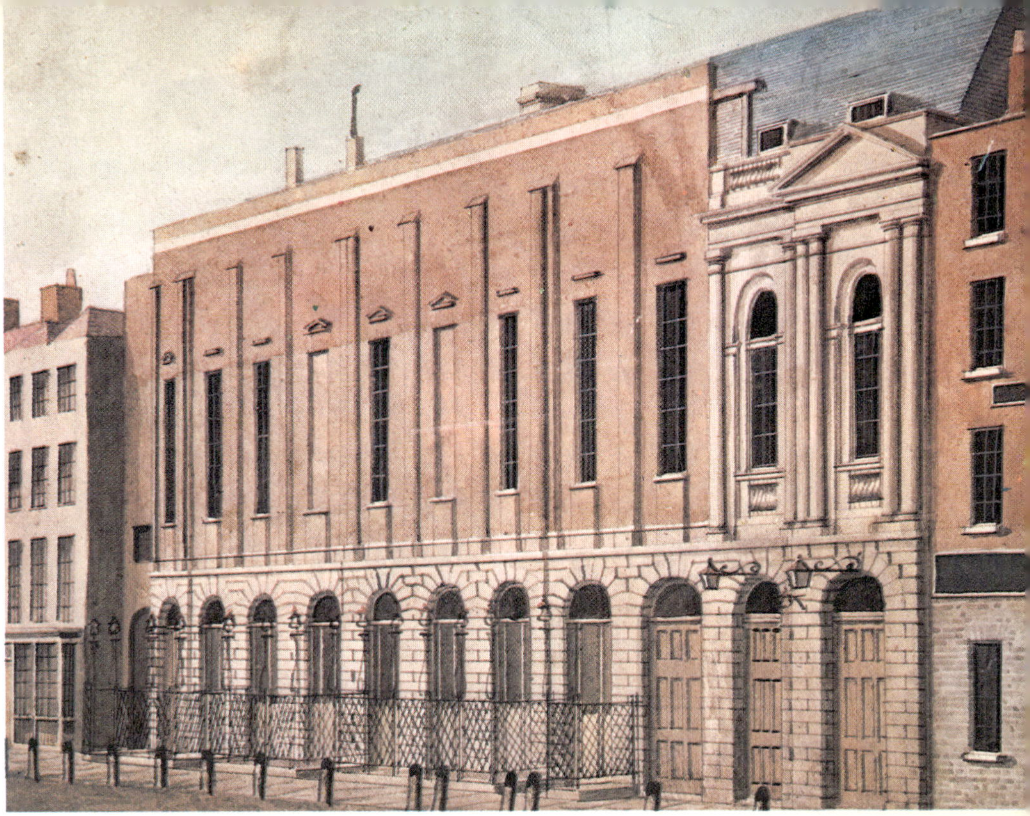

**Above** The New Street looking towards the Quadrant from Rudolf Ackermann's 1822 series of aquatints. On the left can be seen Carbonell & Co.'s premises, designed by Robert Abraham, and then C. R. Cockerell's Archbishop Tenison's Chapel. *Plate III*

**Above left** Looking north from Langham Place and Portland Place about 1822. *Plate IV*

**Left** East Crescent, now part of Park Crescent, from an aquatint by Rudolf Ackermann, 1822. On the right are the railings of Regent's Park, on the left, Portland Place. *Plate V*

**Left** Regent Street, in the 1830s, looking north from Hanover Street, past the Hanover Chapel to Oxford Street and All Souls' Langham Place. *Plate VI*

**Below** St James's Market, about 1840, by C. J. Richardson. The market was rebuilt in 1817 to 1818 by James Burton. It was demolished after the First World War. *Plate VII*

# Regent's Park

'They present to the astonished spectator, so magnificent are the buildings, and so tasteful is the scenery, more the appearance of the newly founded capital of a wealthy state, than one of the suburbs of an ancient city.'

Regent's Park is not really part of Regent Street and was important to Regent Street only in the beginning. Once Regent Street was developed, it could and does stand alone as a shopping street, rather than a major thoroughfare. However, the development of Regent's Park deserves a glance because of the involvement of at least one major developer, and because of the impetus which its development gave to the making of the street.

Development started with Park Crescent, undertaken in 1812 by a man called Mayor, who ran out of money, scared off other speculators, and whose abandoned and unfinished buildings fell down in 1820. It was not till the early 1820s that the two southern quadrants were finished, and that the decision was taken to replace the northern part of the Circus by the two sides of Park Square.

A happier beginning was made by the planting of a large number of trees in the Park as soon as the Commissioners authorised the adoption of a modified version of Nash's plan at the end of 1811.

As Ann Saunders points out in her history of Regent's Park, its development was badly hit by the post-war depression of 1815–19, and it was only built after an heroic struggle. The Crown had no spare capital to lend to builders, as the great private estates often did, so the Park was largely the creation of a number of developers. Forty per cent of the leases were held by eleven individuals.

The most important of these was James Burton, (1761–1837), a man who dominated the north London building scene at the beginning of the nineteenth century. He was an enterprising Scotsman who began his career in Southwark, and then moved into development on the Bedford and Foundling Estates in Bloomsbury in 1800. With a large organisation in Bloomsbury, he was well equipped to undertake operations in Regent's Park and Regent Street, where his developments were almost more extensive. He built a number of important terraces in the Park, including Cornwall Terrace developed in 1821. This was the first terrace to be erected apparently to the design of his young son Decimus (1800–1881).

Cumberland Terrace, in Regent's Park, designed by Nash, and developed by William Mountford Nurse, in 1826.

Burton was largely responsible for the villas in the centre of the Park. The Prince's proposed *guinguette* (a pleasure pavilion) was never built but a number of palatial homes for the nobility and gentry, including one for the Marquess of Hertford, were erected. Burton built himself a classical villa, the Holme, to his son's design in 1818.

Nash designed most of the façades for the terraces, though his design for at least one group, in Gloucester Gate, was altered by the builder's architect. He designed Cumberland Terrace, the grandest terrace in the Park, intended as a key element in the design as it stood opposite the site of the Prince's proposed *guinguette*.

Nash took a number of leases himself, notably eight acres originally intended for the Canal Company on the unfashionable east side of the Park. This proceeding was criticised by the parliamentary committee which investigated the matter, but seems to have been inspired by a feeling of personal responsibility for the success of the venture. When the Canal Company jibbed he took on the area, and seems to have made a reasonable financial success out of it. The earth excavated from the Canal Basin was used to make some eleven million bricks, many of which were used in Regent Street. The land was developed as wharves and commercial buildings round the Basin, and as working-class housing in Augustus Street. Nash was also directly responsible for the somewhat unorthodox development of *cottages ornés* in Park Village, a group harking back to his work at Blaise Hamlet in 1811. Its rural atmosphere must have been considerably heightened by the Canal with horse-drawn barges at the bottom of the gardens.

The Canal was, of course, not only ornamental—it was an important means of transport, both for the markets on the east of the Park, and for builders' materials for those developing the Park and for Regent Street itself.

Mogg's plan of 1828 shows the Park as developed, complete with terraces and villas in the Park, more modest cottages, and terraces of working-class housing on the eastern fringes. Here lay the Canal basin and the conveniently situated market. Of the three markets projected only one was built—Cumberland Market, to which the Haymarket was transferred from St James's in 1830. An enormous icehouse was built underneath it, something for which the soil of Camden Town was thought to be particularly well suited.

A few selected public buildings were allowed in the Park itself. The most spectacular was the Colosseum, designed by Decimus Burton to house a panorama of London, painted from sketches made from the dome of St Paul's Cathedral, and erected in the inside of a domed building to give less intrepid climbers the same thrill. (Plate XVII)

The original elevating concept was supplemented by other entertainments, and by 1855 included the inevitable Swiss Cottage, a museum of sculpture, stalactite-filled caverns and a conservatory.

Slightly further south in the Park, on the east side of Park Square, was another place of entertainment, the Diorama, in which an elaborate magic lantern show was used to display paintings of architectural and romantic subjects.

One of the first and most enduring tenants in

**Left** View from Wellin's Farm, Marybone Park, towards Highgate in 1799.
**Right** Regent's Park in 1828.
**Bottom right** The Colosseum, Regent's Park, looking towards the south in 1846. It was demolished in 1875. See Plate XVII
**Bottom left** The Holme, James Burton's villa in Regent's Park, now part of Bedford College.

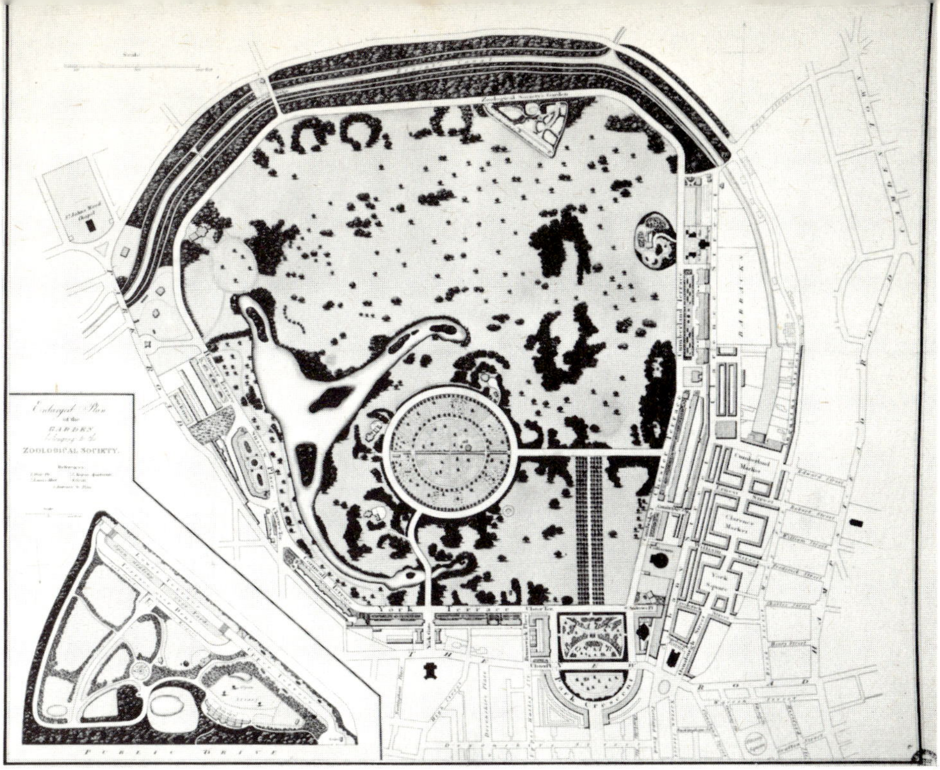

the Park was the Zoological Society of London, probably the best known place of public entertainment in the Park, if not in all London. After some discussion the Society was allotted 20 acres on the northern edge of the Park. It appointed Decimus Burton architect and the zoo very soon became one of the sights of the metropolis. Two years after it was established the zoo acquired its first elephant, and in 1836 Burton designed a house for the first giraffes.

Immediate contemporaries of Nash were enthusiastic:

'See the rich embroidered prospect now before us! Look on our right how the huge cupola of the Coliseum spreads its ample rotunda among the groves of mansions, pleasure grounds and squares. See the bizarre minarets of Sussex Place on our left, . . . and the tasteful pilasters of Cornwall Terrace. . . .'

Public appreciation of Nash's work fell sharply soon after his death—the sour words of John Murray writing in 1843 are a fair sample:

'. . . wherever the hand of Mr John Nash is manifest, beauty is at once exchanged for artificial littleness, as in his greater and lesser circuses, his ornamental bridges over puddles four feet wide, his Swiss cottages, and his terraces crowned with cupolas, that convey to the mind of the spectator the idea of a grotesque giant in his dressing gown and nightcap.'

The Regent's Park terraces gradually declined in public appreciation, reaching their nadir during the Second World War when the Crown Estate Commissioners, the ground landlords, decided against running repairs on the bombed houses, because they planned total redevelopment after the war. Fortunately, this scheme was prevented, and the terraces have now been repaired and in some cases totally rebuilt—a great salvage operation to set against much of the post-war vandalism in London.

Today, perhaps, we are more appreciative of Nash's romantic panorama. It is essentially theatrical architecture, a grand back-drop to the important social lives of the residents, and of course, a permanent contribution to London. The Regent's Park has always had its share of grand residents, but it never became as important, as royal or as glamorous as Nash had intended. It was perhaps a little too retired, too distant from Westminster and St James's to compete with Mayfair or even Belgravia.

**Above** Park Village East, Regent's Park, from the Canal towpath in 1827

**Left** The Zoological Gardens in 1851.

## Lower Regent Street to Waterloo Place

Development started at the St James's Park end of the new street, partly because most of the property there belonged to the Crown anyway (See Plate IX), and partly because development there was under the very windows of Carlton House. Early in 1816 demolition of the houses west of the Haymarket in Market Lane and St James's Market began, and was followed by the total erasure of St Albans Street, and the removal of the Market to a smaller site, immediately west of the Haymarket. Nash was most insistent that a new market should be built. 'It has been at least understood' he pointed out, 'that a new Market should be substituted—open shambles are essential to the poor and the poorer description of tradesmen who cannot pay large rents.'

Round the market were a number of small houses for tradesmen: a builder, a plumber, a tailor, a carpenter and joiner—an important element in the comprehensive planning of the area which was to make it such a success. As in Regent's Park, where a large area to the east had been provided for domestic marketing and the service industries, so in the rich area of the Haymarket and Lower Regent Street, Nash still took care that there should be room for artisans and small shopkeepers. (See Plate VII).

Waterloo Place and Lower Regent Street had a smart residential character which was missing from the centre portion of the street. Charles Tufton Blicke built a grand mansion at No. 15, though it is perhaps significant that it was replaced in 1838 by Decimus Burton's Club Chambers.

Opposite No. 15 Nash designed a very grand block containing his own house and one for John Edwards, his mysterious cousin, with whom he was involved in speculation in Suffolk Street. The house was much more like an Italian palazzo than a London terrace house. On the ground floor there were shops on to the street, entrances within the court for the two residences, and then offices, with stables behind, approached from Market Street. Above this were two interlocking maisonettes, that of Nash serving both as home and office. His apartments were dominated by a long gallery, decorated with specially commissioned copies of Raphael's work at the Vatican, and with copies of the Apollo Belvedere and other well known classical statues. There was also a collection of models of the most important classical buildings, made in Paris to Nash's order. This gallery served both as a reception room for entertainments and as a study for Nash, while there was a drawing office for clerks at the back of the building. The house must have made a convenient centre for operations, where he could watch the gradual progress of his new street, or from which he could walk across the Park to his equally grand but perhaps less immediately successful and popular extension to Buckingham Palace.

On the whole, however, it was not a family street, and hotels, clubs and chambers were the order of the day. Mr Warren, whose hotel dominated the south-eastern corner of the street, was an old Crown tenant, who had moved from Charles Street. Though the hotel was patronised by the nobility and higher clergy in its early days, it gradually acquired a racier reputation. It was reconstructed in 1848, and re-christened the Maurigy, then the Continental. With a change in name came a change in character, until in 1906 it was closed down by the police, after a raid which caused a certain amount of embarrassment in society.

Carlton Chambers at Nos. 4–12, opposite the hotel, were designed by Burton, and served both as offices and bachelor lodgings. Decimus Burton, James' successful architect son, had his office there, and there was a long tradition of architectural practices, including William Railton, designer of the Nelson Monument in Trafalgar Square, and George Gilbert Scott. There were also a number of solicitors, emphasising the relatively quiet professional character of the street compared with the bustling commerce north of the Circus.

Nash was keenly aware of the importance of capturing leaders of fashion, and one of his first successes was the sale of an important plot on the corner of Charles Street to the United Service Club, one of the first 'members' Clubs' in London. The founding members took the site in May 1816, having appointed Robert Smirke as their architect. The brief and the budget were both modest and Smirke produced a 'frigid design, somewhat

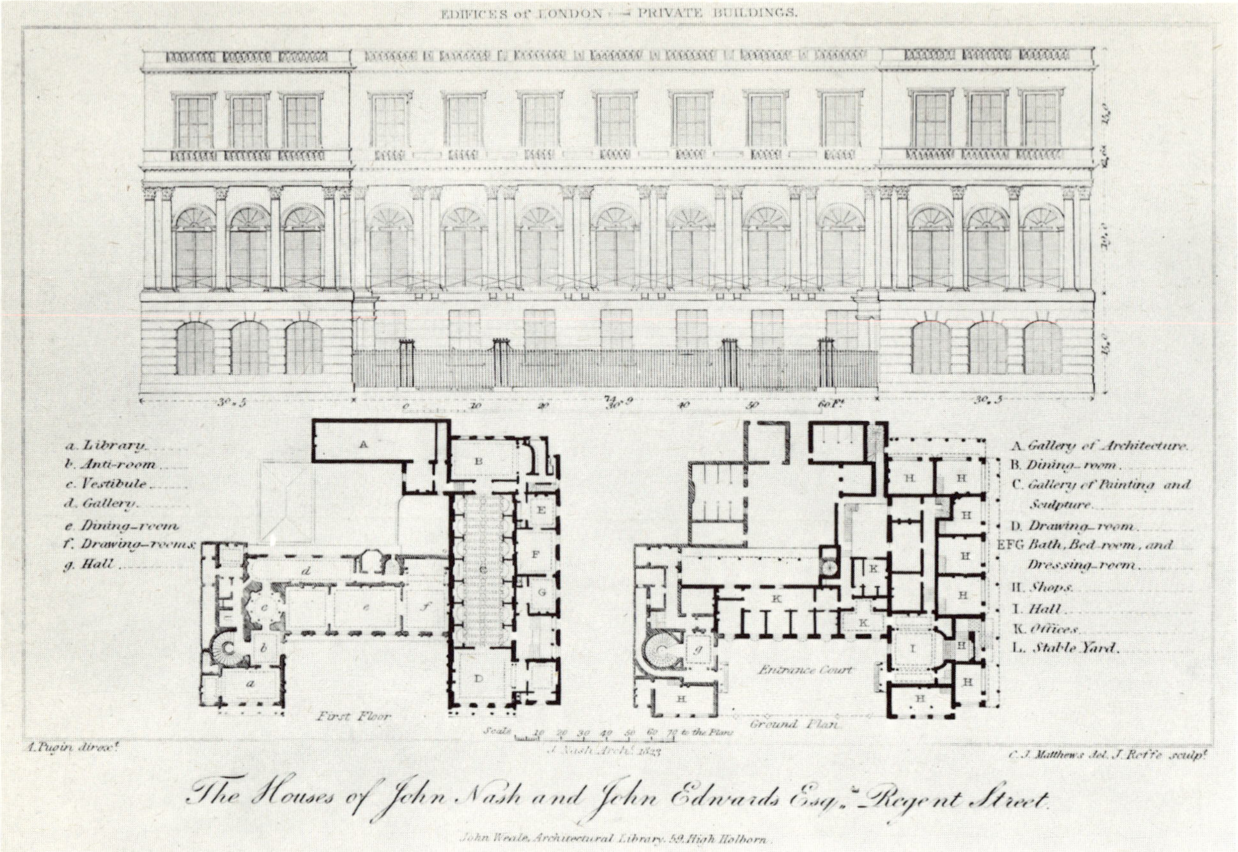


Nos. 14 and 16 Regent Street in 1823. No. 14 was Nash's own house. After his death his house was divided up, part becoming chambers, and part the famous gallery, the Gallery of Illustrations.

relieved by sculpture on the entrance front, of Britannia distributing laurels to her brave sons by land and sea'. Internally it was also very plain and seems to have been too small, and when Carlton House opposite was demolished the Committee applied for the magnificent site on the corner of Pall Mall and Waterloo Place. In 1826 the Committee decided to sell the existing clubhouse and build a new one. Significantly, they decided to employ Nash rather than Smirke again.

Fortunately for the members, the old clubhouse was bought by the newly formed Junior Club, founded to accommodate junior officers. They also found the building too small, and employed Burton to carry out extensive alterations in 1830. These were still unsatisfactory, and in 1854 the Club bought some adjoining houses, and employed T. Marsh Nelson to design an enlarged clubhouse. Outside, imposing Bath stone elevations replaced Smirke's stucco, while inside the increased influence and sophistication of mid-Victorian club life was reflected in a larger number of rooms. Smirke's austerity was replaced by greater ornateness and elaboration influenced, according to one account, by the Viennese baroque of Fischer von Erlach. The Junior United Service Club's progress reflects that of West End club life in general: in 1903–4 the servants' accommodation was improved and in 1915 members' bedrooms and bathrooms and a ladies' dining-room were added. In 1952, however, the United Service Club was persuaded to open its doors to junior officers, and the two clubs amalgamated, leaving the Junior Clubhouse to the house-breakers.

The bottom of Waterloo Place is dominated by Nash's United Service Club and Decimus Burton's

**Top** The Gallery of Nash's house.

**Right** Club Chambers, No. 15 Regent Street, designed and built by Decimus Burton.

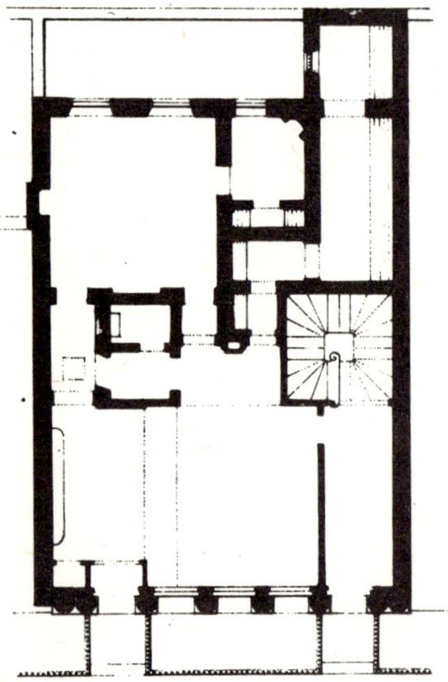

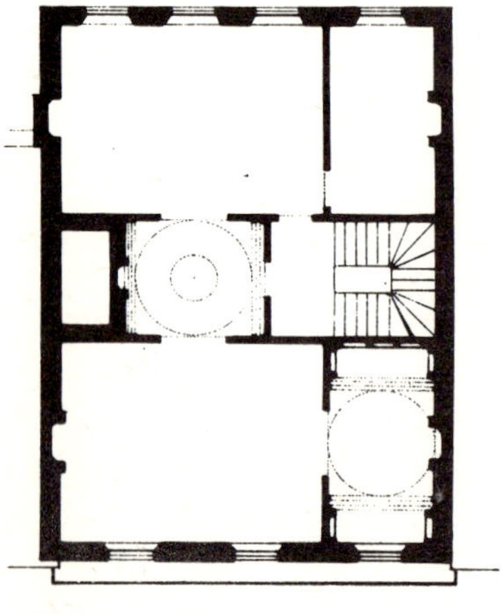

Athenaeum Clubhouse, balancing compositions but not, as they were intended, of a 'common design'. The Commissioners of Woods and Forests when granting a lease to the Athenaeum stipulated that the facing façades 'should be made to correspond in every respect'.

Burton, in designing the Athenaeum, was to comply with Nash's design for the United Service Club which had taken its lease earlier. However, owing to some confusion and considerable disingenuousness on the part of Nash, who as architect to both the United Service Club and the Commissioners should have behaved rather better, the design for the older club was changed at the last minute. This left the Athenaeum with a continuous first-floor balcony, while the other club had a double portico on the north. In fact, the difference between the two buildings is not aggressive, and they are both elegant and important compositions in their own right, so perhaps the lack of uniformity does not matter.

After Carlton House was demolished, Nash designed the two wings of Carlton House Terrace to overlook the Mall, originally planned with no entrance to the Park from Waterloo Place. This was partly to accommodate one of his more fantastic projects—a temple using the old columns from Carlton House, containing a fountain. The object, as he explained, was to supply a replacement for the old portico at Carlton House, which would be missed by everyone coming down the street. '. . . speaking as a painter it will improve the view, and being an open Temple, you will see the Park between the columns in a most picturesque manner.' In the event, this was not carried out, and Waterloo Place was terminated by the Duke of York's column, erected in 1833.

In the Haymarket Nash carried out some of his most successful schemes. With Repton he designed a new front for the Opera House which had been left a sad mess by Novosielski and Leverton, (see Plate II). The Opera House was arcaded on all sides, the western arcade between it and the backs of houses in Waterloo Place becoming London's first shopping arcade. This was copied from Paris and was to become the forerunner of a number of London's most elegant and intimate shopping streets. On the other side of the Haymarket, Nash persuaded the owner of the Little Theatre, David Morris, to rebuild on the axis of Charles Street, so as to close the vista eastwards from St James's Square. The theatre occupied a long narrow site running back into Suffolk Street.

**Above** Athenaeum Club, Pall Mall.
**Right** The Opera House, Haymarket, as completed by John Nash. The Royal Opera Arcade, now the only survival of Nash's work on the site, was part of the development, and there were also some shops in the colonnade.
**Left** The Banking House of Messrs Hopkinson at No. 3, Lower Regent Street, again designed by Repton. The brothers George, Caesar, Charles and Edmund Hopkinson were established in their new premises as bankers and army agents in 1820. Their bank remained at No. 3 until the early years of this century after being absorbed by Prescott's Bank.

Nash was involved in Suffolk Street himself to such a degree that the Select Committee on Crown Leases of 1829 looked into the matter very carefully, concluding, however, that Nash had behaved perfectly properly. The sites in question were originally taken by his 'relation and friend' John Edwards in 1800. Edwards was a former solicitor, who wished to undertake development on a system common at the time. 'I intended,' he explained, 'to have advanced builders money, taking the carcasses of the houses as my security of five per cent, and charging an additional ground rent, which would have been worth so many years' purchase.' After two years Nash took it off his hands, partly to oblige Edwards, partly it would seem because he felt that Edwards was not ready 'to lay out a large sum to make it a good thing in building'.

Thus Nash became the head lessee of all the land on the east side, and much on the west. This was hardly a gilt-edged investment—in the dry words of John Shaw, a leading architect and surveyor to Christ's Hospital: 'Suffolk Street was a very abominable street, and it was a matter of opinion whether this intended speculation could purify its character'.

Considerable impetus was given to its development by the building of the University Clubhouse on the corner of Pall Mall at No. 1 Suffolk Street, in 1823, to the design of William Wilkins (1778–1839), the architect of the National Gallery, and J. P. Gandy-Deering (1787–1850). This followed Nash's chosen pattern of public buildings on key sites.

The layout of the rest of the street shows Nash's ingenuity at its most fertile. He had to minimise the disadvantage of the shallow site on the east backing on to the seedy Dorset Place, and this was done by letting the ground floor, with a Dorset Place frontage for use as cellars, to Paxton, an important wine merchant, and to other locals for stabling. Above this a large toplit gallery with a minimal frontage to Suffolk Street was leased to the Royal Society of British Artists, at No. 6½. This left the Suffolk Street frontage open for development, mostly by other architects, including George Ledwell Taylor, architect of Morley's Hotel in Trafalgar Square (Nos. 4 and 5), and Lewis Wyatt, nephew of the great Surveyor-General James Wyatt, (Nos. 12–14).

Equally typical of Nash was the organisation of the façades, so that the Ionic portico of Price's

Italian warehouse closed the vista from the Haymarket up Suffolk Place, as did the more modest Garland's Hotel, at No. 16, for the view from Pall Mall. This hotel, together with Nos. 1–5 Suffolk Place, the only remaining complete Nash block in the street, was destroyed in the Second World War.

The top end of Lower Regent Street became more commercial as it approached the Circus, and even Mr Gledstane's house, designed at the same time as St Philip's Chapel by G. S. Repton, had a lock-up shop in the front.

North of Jermyn Street, the elegant matching façades were designed as an introduction to Regent Circus South. Both sides up to and including the southern quadrants were taken by a developer called Frisby Howis, and completed in about 1817.

Regent Circus South must have demonstrated Nash's skill in crossing major roads 'imperceptibly' more clearly than the northern circus. Views up Lower Regent Street (see page 33) show how elegantly this was achieved.

Piccadilly had been an important coaching centre, and even after the railways had superseded the stage coach, there were services to and from the northern termini for both parcels and people. This explains the large number of coach and railway offices in the Circus itself.

The County Fire Office dominates the whole of Lower Regent Street. It is an extremely cleverly planned building on a difficult narrow site left by the junction of Regent Street and Marylebone Street. Its dramatic façade is clearly influenced by that of Inigo Jones's old Somerset House, and Summerson suggests that Nash as a young man living in Lambeth would have had time to study the facade. Thus, though Robert Abraham was the County Fire Insurance Company's architect, it was probably Nash who was instrumental in choosing the design.

**Left** The Theatre Royal, Haymarket, 1821. It was rebuilt to Nash's elevation, and upon a site chosen by him, to provide a fitting terminus to the new eastern portion of Charles Street opened into the Haymarket from Lower Regent Street.
**Right** The County Fire Office from Lower Regent Street. This photograph, taken some time between 1854, when Nelson's new clubhouse was erected, and 1885, when the north-east quadrant was removed, shows very clearly Nash's genius for handling vistas. Whether it is the important views in the grand streets, past the Quadrant to Vigo House, up Regent Street itself to All Souls' Church, or the modest streets like Suffolk Street, or even Suffolk Place off the Haymarket, there was always something well contrived at the end of a Nash street to catch the eye and concentrate the attention.

# Regent Street and Piccadilly Circus

The disruption to the normal commercial life of the area close to the new street was enormous. Nowhere was it worse than in the area around Piccadilly. The story as told in the sober pages of the ratebooks is very clear. In that part of St James's Parish north of Piccadilly, and to the western side of the new street, the Commissioners demolished nearly 250 houses—20 where the new street crossed Piccadilly, the same number in Jermyn Street, over 40 houses in Vine and Glasshouse Streets, and of course, the majority of Swallow Street itself, leaving a few aristocratic stables at the Piccadilly end, and about ten houses in Swallow Passage at the north.

Trade was horribly disrupted – shops were pulled down, customers displaced, access became difficult and uninviting and no street cleansing or maintenance was carried out. The Commissioners did their best to minimise the inconvenience and, of course, they paid the poor rate to compensate the parish for the empty houses. Compulsorily purchased houses were left occupied as long as possible; existing tenants were given the first chance to purchase a new lease, even to undertake redevelopment, except where they were undesirable, as in 'abominable' Suffolk Street, where new leaseholders were found in an attempt to raise the tone of the area.

Familiar names can be seen emerging in the new street. The Charles Street hotel keeper, William Warren, built a grand new hotel in Lower Regent Street. Newman, a substantial stable-keeper in Swallow Street, was among the last to be displaced. He had a fine new mews built and a postmaster's business at No. 121, with an exit into Regent Street, but also rebuilt some of the houses in Regent Street itself, including the distinctive domed corner house at No. 115. In Piccadilly George Swan, a Ludgate Hill shopkeeper, had opened a shop at No. 20 in 1814, but this was in the way of the Circus, and by 1820 his shop was swept away. However, he took on Nos. 9 and 10 the following year, and this, far from being an unforeseen disaster, may have been a shrewd business move, a method of ensuring a prime site in the new street. Unfortunately, he did not survive the move long, dying in 1821 and leaving the

**Left** A Street View, from Marylebone Street, Golden Square, towards Regent Street.
**Left** A view looking from Coventry Street towards Regent Street.
**Right** A view looking from Piccadilly towards Air Street, Regent Street.

These three views of the new development were all sold by Smith and Warner, one of the many firms who had to deal with the problem of retaining their old customers at a new address, in a totally redeveloped neighbourhood.

R. Havell Aqua.

*A Street View shewing part of the Improvement of London, and Leading to*
SMITH (late SMITH & WARNERS) New Superfine Colour Manufactory
*Removed from 208, Piccadilly,* to No. 34, Marylebone Street, Piccadilly,
at the back of and next to the County Fire Office.
*the above is a View from His late Shew Room in Piccadilly, looking up Air Street, and Shewing part of the Regents Quadrant and Marylebone Street, in the extreme distance to which He is Removed as above stated.*

business to his young assistant, William Edgar. The effect of the move was clearly beneficial, as Swan and Edgar's first year's sales were over £80,000.

In general, the effect of the redevelopment was to raise the standard of the area, and this again is supported by evidence from the ratebooks. In the Church division of St James's Parish, by 1824, when redevelopment was almost complete, the rates had been raised by over £1000 to £2,279, an increase which reflected the rise in rental from £7,708 to £13,676.

Such a large redevelopment obviously took time, and completion was patchy in the main stretch of Regent Street itself, possibly most difficult in the Quadrant, where the ominous word 'bankrupt' appeared occasionally. Even when the rates were paid, this was sometimes done by the builders themselves as in 1825, at Nos. 98 and 100, when May and Morritt, a well known firm of iron-mongers, were down in the ratebooks as the occupiers and rate payers.

The first residents on the west side of the street, near Conduit Street where stood the last part of Swallow Street to be demolished, moved in in 1823. They included Thomas Reid, a bread and biscuit baker, one of the few food shopkeepers in the street, at No. 227; Mrs Elizabeth Fox and Son, woollen-drapers (and silk mercers) at No. 203; Robert Lendrum, tailor and habit-maker, at No. 225; and, at No. 215, John Purkis, Professor of Music, who went bankrupt a few years later.

The street filled up rapidly in the next few years, with the occasional house remaining empty. Those erected expressly by businesses for their own occupation were filled up first—thus the wine merchant J. Carbonell was established by 1825, and the northern circus saw the establishment of the substantial pioneers, Hodge and Lowman, at Nos. 252–4. On the whole, however, even where a shopkeeper owned more than one site, the shop occupying a single frontage was the rule. Little amalgamation either architectural or structural took place. The houses in the new Regent Street were clearly larger and more valuable than those in the old Swallow Street, but the shops were still modest. It is difficult to assess the actual change in the number of people living in the area for, though a

**Left** The demolition of Swallow Street, 1821.
**Centre** William Edgar.
**Above** Regent Street, Drawing Room Day, 1851. This is one of a series published by Rudolph Ackermann, Junior, for sale to visitors to the Great Exhibition. This print shows the Band of the Life Guards proceeding to Buckingham Palace, naturally at the moment when they pass Ackermann's own shop. He was one of the original lessees in Regent Street, setting up at No. 191 in 1826, separately from his father's well-known establishment in the Strand. Next door is the original shop of Lewis and Allenby, silk mercers, later to build one of the first purpose-built stores in Conduit Street.

larger number of small houses were demolished, the new houses were all larger houses with provision for living accommodation in the upper storeys.

Within ten years of the street's virtual completion, in 1835, a hard-headed investigation into paving rates concluded that the success of Regent Street was now proved. The rental of houses in the street itself had risen by about a third, and it had enhanced the value of all property in the streets near it in the parishes of St James's and St George's. Interestingly it had done more for gentlemen's houses than tradesmen's, and perhaps not unexpectedly the investigation concluded that Bond Street had suffered somewhat, confirming a French traveller's later verdict: '*Regent-street, rue qui, d'une percée recente, a succèdé, sous le rapport de l'élégance, a Bond-street, ancien théâtre des dandys et du beau monde, ainsi que des courtisanes.*'

Regent Street was a very bold piece of town planning; it was also bold to the point of foolhardiness as far as normal commercial practice went. In 'bringing an unusual quantity of land into the market' the Commissioners of Woods and Forests gave Nash a very difficult task, in which he would have failed without the assistance of two important builders, and his own readiness to adopt bold and unorthodox solutions.

The first builder was Samuel Baxter of Carmarthen Street, Tottenham Court Road, who took all four crescents of Regent Circus North as well as odd houses south of Piccadilly. He was one of the three builders who rescued Park Crescent in 1818, and was a major developer in Regent's Park. He was not as fashionable or perhaps as educated a man as James Burton, but seems to have been influential, and capable.

James Burton is, however, the man to whom, after Nash, Regent Street owes most. Alexander Milne (*c.* 1781–1861), the experienced civil servant who was secretary to the New Street Commissioners, said that but for Burton, it would have been difficult to get rid of all the building ground, thus paying tribute to Burton's readiness to come to the rescue. This readiness was based perhaps on a knowledge of how much he would lose should public confidence in the street be shaken, and the progress halted. It was due to Nash and Burton that Regent Street was effectively completed before the building slump of the late 1820s.

Even James Burton's commercial courage failed at the prospect of the Quadrant; only Nash, in Summerson's words, was 'rich enough or rash enough' to undertake the Quadrant. Over sixty houses were involved on both sides, and the effect of his great sweep could easily have been destroyed by incompetent setting out, or by the unhappy junction between two different builders' work. Even his position as Commissioners' architect was not enough, he felt, to give him adequate powers of coordination, so he undertook the development of the whole Quadrant himself.

By a complicated series of deals with various master-tradesmen, he paid them for their work by assigning the leases of the completed houses and shops to them or their nominees. In addition, he advanced money to them to meet any shortage of cash while building was in progress. He estimated that he had advanced a total of £60,000. Neither of these two systems was exactly new, but Nash used them in a very sophisticated way to complete the Quadrant in two years, 1819 and 1820.

Nash had planned well: the great sweep of the Quadrant is the gateway to Regent Street, and had this failed or jarred in any way the whole enterprise would have been in jeopardy. Further north, it was not essential that each block should read as a unity, and where individual 'takes' were not big enough he seems to have been happy to fill in with smaller houses. Nash claimed to have been responsible for all the elevations of the new street but, when pressed by a parliamentary committee, had to admit that Soane, Smirke and others had contributed designs. '. . . but,' he added somewhat ungraciously, 'submitted by the Office for my opinion; if a person presents a design for the elevation of a building, and I do not see a material defect, it would be invidious of me to find fault with it.'

The result of this system was, in purist architectural eyes, uneven. James Elmes, normally an admirer of Nash, summed it up:

'Therefore, . . . with all these merits, I consider Regent Street to possess many blemishes; some of the architectural specimens being in a taste absolutely barbarous, and mixed with others equally pure and refined. Its masses, great parts and divisions, are grand and effective; and its breaks and general outline productive of an agreeable variety of light and shade, while at the same time it is entirely free from that dull monotony of elevation which is so wearisome in many of our new streets.'

No less than five of the largest blocks were taken by the brave and indefatigable Burton including almost the whole of the street from Vigo Street to Conduit Street on the west, and the lower east side from the Quadrant to Beak Street. The block next to Beak Street was the only one in the street let by public tender—Burton had to compete with Edwards and Robins, a local estate agent. Elsewhere in the street the problem seems to have been to find takers.

There were two impressive pedimented and pilastered blocks, Nos. 132–154, later Chesham House, on the east side (see page 96), and an even longer block, Nos. 171–195 on the west side, between New Burlington and Conduit Streets (page 105). Perhaps most agreeable as street architecture was the block between Leicester Street and New Burlington Street, Nos. 133–167, with its modest seven-bay central block with a square attic, and slightly recessed wings with mansards behind an elegant pierced stucco parapet.

It is not clear who designed these blocks. It seems possible that it was Decimus Burton, then still a very young man, but one who was credited with designing his father's villa in Regent's Park at the age of 18. These blocks were leased, and therefore almost completed, but not necessarily let, between 1820 and 1823, so this is not out of the question. Certainly they seem to owe more to Burton than to Nash, though we cannot deny Nash his overall supervision.

The most distinguished block in the street was that between Chapel Street and Beak Street, designed by Sir John Soane for J. Robins, the estate agent, and finished in 1820. Sir John Soane was then professor of architecture at the Royal Academy, as well as architect to the Bank of England, and this, his largest piece of 'domestic architecture', to use Elmes's term, caused considerable interest. Its simple elegance was set off by classical figures on the skyline. It is unusual in that it caused a lawsuit: an unfriendly review suggesting that Soane had invented a new classical order provoked him to sue the journalist for libel.

The area round Oxford Circus was almost totally dominated by Baxter. The Circus itself with its Corinthian arcades was presumably designed by Nash, but it would be interesting to know who provided the design for Nos. 224–240. This seems very influenced by Soane, but it is so heavily handled that one is reminded of Nash's complaint about the way that builders never stuck to the drawings provided.

The sole survivor of old Swallow Street was Archbishop Tenison's Chapel, founded in 1687, rebuilt in 1702, and protected by the New Street Act from disturbance. The early eighteenth century building was given a new stone façade by C. R. Cockerell (1788–1863), but this did not survive for long. In 1854 the trustees of the chapel rebuilt their street frontage and let it to a shop.

Cockerell also designed the other church in this part of Regent Street, St George's Chapel, or the Hanover Chapel, as it was known. Its massive stone portico and its characteristic square towers were well-known landmarks in the street, (see Plate No. XII).

Regent Street, looking south from the Hanover Chapel, about 1890. On the left are Nos. 224–240, in Elmes's words 'as picturesque a range of buildings as any between Portland Place and Pall Mall', later the premises of Dickins and Jones.

**Above** The Harmonic Institution, Regent Street, in 1828.
**Left** The Hanover Chapel, designed by C.R. Cockerell, consecrated in 1825, was an important landmark at the northern end of Regent Street until its demolition in 1897.
**Top right** Nos. 132–154, on the east side of Regent Street, developed by James Burton, possibly designed by Decimus Burton. The number on Gedge's premises should be 132 not 123. The block was later known as Chesham House.
**Right** Nos. 156–170, on the east side of Regent Street, designed by Sir John Soane.

REGENT STREET
REGENT STREET
R BURTON

REGENT STREET
123

Across the street stood one of the best known public buildings, the Harmonic Institution. This was originally a wing of the mansion house of the second Duke of Argyll. In 1806 it was opened as a place of entertainment, first known as the 'Fashionable Institution', then the Argyll Rooms, by H. F. Greville, a well-known rake and man-about-town. It survived until 1813, with dwindling popularity, but in that year was opened as the headquarters of a musical society, which was to stage a series of subscription concerts, thus starting a musical tradition. This was to give Regent Street a strong musical flavour throughout the century. In 1818 the rooms were rebuilt as part of the new street scheme to the design of Nash for another musical society, which obtained royal patronage as the Royal Harmonic Institution. However, not all its functions were subscription concerts, as a cartoon by Cruikshank of the Cyprians' Ball in 1825 makes clear.

Despite an awkward site Nash provided a characteristically ingenious solution—the main concert room was placed on the eastern edge of the site, leaving the Regent Street frontage free for shops, and room for other public rooms on the first floor. On the corner was a domed building which solved the architectural problem of the acute angle between Little Argyll Street and Regent Street.

By 1822 the society was in low water, and only two members remained to carry on the Rooms. Despite their troubles, however, the concerts were kept going, attracting such distinguished musicians as Liszt, Mendelssohn and Weber. In 1830 the Rooms were burnt down, a common fate for theatres and places of entertainment, and the society moved its concerts to the Hanover Square Rooms, and then to the St James's Hall. The Rooms were rebuilt as houses and shops, but the musical tradition of Regent Street survived their departure, as George Sala described in 1859: 'Music hath charms in Regent Street; and its paving-stones unceasingly echo beneath the feet of the denizens of the musical world.' Regent Street was for the musical lion as Tattersall's was for the horsey celebrity.

**Right** Regent Circus, Oxford Street, in 1850 with All Souls' Church behind, Jay's Mourning Warehouse on the left, and the Life Guards in the foreground.
**Below** The Regent Street Polytechnic.

# Upper Regent Street

Upper Regent Street was planned to run southward in a straight line from Portland Place, but circumstances were against Nash. He was, as he complained, 'shoved to the eastward' by the owners of the Cavendish Square houses, and in the course of one of the most famous rows between client and architect ever recorded, he decided to take the street further east still.

He bought Foley House from Lord Foley, an old client who already owed him money, pulled it down and drove the new sewer through the site ready for building. He sold the site on the west, in line with the west side of Portland Place, to Sir James Langham on the understanding that he would be employed to build a new, smaller, but still substantial town house. Unfortunately, this house started giving trouble, and Sir James called in another architect. The mortified Nash took his revenge and threatened to lay out his street so that Sir James's house was overlooked by the backs of houses on the west side of Upper Regent Street. There was no way out—the unhappy baronet paid heavily, both for the plot to the east and for having insulted Nash!

**Above** North front of Langham House in 1844. This was built by Nash on part of the site of Foley House, Portland Place. It was demolished in 1864 for the building of the Langham Hotel. See page 87.

A new church was needed for the district, and Nash sited it at the top of the new street, planning its much-ridiculed spire, set inappropriately on a circular portico, to act as an eye-catcher for passers-by turning the corner, as well as for those coming up Regent Street itself. Over two-thirds of the cost of the church, some £20,000, was contributed by the Commissioners for Building New Churches, and thanks to its siting near the wealthy Cavendish Square it became a very fashionable church. George IV contributed the altarpiece as a mark of approbation to his architect, though whether it compensated Nash for the unkind parliamentary remarks about his spire is arguable. By the time that the cartoon of him astride his church appeared, the opposition to George IV was becoming increasingly vocal, and the royal architect was of course, a convenient substitute for the royal patron. (See Plate VIII).

The top end of Regent Street was, in Elmes's happy phrase, 'the isthmus between wealth and commerce', and largely built with small houses which might serve for either, without offending the rich inhabitants of Portland Place and Harley Street, then not doctors but nabobs. Despite the relatively modest size of the establishments, Nash was still vigilant, and even Mr Marks's coachbuilding establishment on the corner of Riding House street had a carefully contrived architectural façade, worthy to stand beside the church. West of the church, on the site of Broadcasting House, Nash designed a correct and agreeable group of four houses.

South of Margaret Street there was little ambiguity—the two blocks between Margaret Street and Great Castle Street were developed by Samuel Baxter, and seem to have been intended for shops rather than for private houses. Nash designed them alike, presumably to provide an architectural coda from the rather miscellaneous character of Langham Place and the upper part of the street to the classical uniformity of the Circus itself.

Nash's carefully contrived street is no longer with us, and such photographs and prints as remain cannot give us the essential three-dimensional quality. It was probably the only great London thoroughfare, with the exception of the post-Fire Cheapside, which was deliberately planned for shopping. It was immensely successful—in the words of an architectural critic, who saw it before its demise in the 1920s, 'a classic example of commercial building'.

It was a stucco street—that easily despised but agreeable, versatile and durable London finish, which meant that every four years the street came out in a gleaming coat of fresh paint. Even its façades were designed for trade, for behind the shopfronts the walls were carried on cast-iron columns so that the frontage could be varied to suit the demands of fashion.

Foreigners who saw the newly completed street were suitably impressed with its bright new architecture and its fashionable shop-windows, set off by the elegant carriages of the rich waiting outside. Ironically, however, even those who made the contemporary crack about the 'nation of shopkeepers' did not see Nash's improvements as

primarily commercial. For the tourist Prince Puckler Muskau it was an enhancement of the whole city: 'London is, however, extremely improved in the direction of Regent Street, Portland Place, and the Regent's Park. Now, for the first time, it has the air of a seat of government . . . Although poor Mr Nash has fared so ill at the hands of connoisseurs . . . yet the country is much indebted to him for conceiving and executing such gigantic designs.'

**Top left** All Souls' Langham Place in 1825, from Upper Regent Street. Behind the symmetrical block on the west side of Langham Place can be seen the chimneys of Langham House.

**Top right** Langham Place, looking north, about 1845. A very early photograph by W.H. Fox-Talbot (1800–1877), one of the pioneers of photography.

**Above** Regent Street from the Quadrant.

# 'A grand commanding street'

## Tallis's Views of Regent Street

John Tallis's Street Views of London were published in part form, one edition in 1838–1840, and a much smaller revised edition in 1847, from which the following views of Regent Street come. Tallis admired Regent Street describing it in 1838, as a 'noble street' whose buildings 'consist chiefly of palace-like shops, in whose broad showy windows are displayed articles of the most splendid description, such as the neighbouring world of wealth and fashion are daily in want of . . . This street possesses, as a whole, a grand and commanding character, and has more architectural features and variety, than any large work witnessed since the rebuilding of London after the great fire . . . it should be visited on a summer's day in the afternoon, when the splendid carriages, and elegantly attired pedestrians, evince the opulence and taste of our magnificent metropolis . . . '

**Waterloo Place and part of Lower Regent Street**
Waterloo Place was designed to form a *place* in front of Carlton House, and its two pilastered sides were intended to set off the view up Lower Regent Street to the Fire Office. In the event they were built as private houses, but an early drawing by Repton for Nos. 1 and 2 shows a plan that could have been used as a shop,

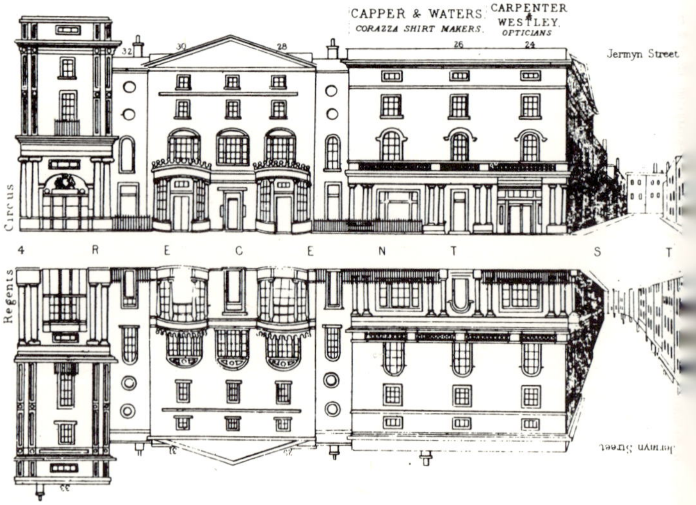


**Lower Regent Street—Upper**
On the west side, next to St Philip's Episcopal Chapel, stood No. 11, designed by Repton for Gledstanes the wine merchants. Like many houses throughout Regent Street, it had a lock-up shop, and a separate house door. It remained as a wine merchants till 1910. It was the last part of Nash's street to be demolished, in 1938. Club Chambers,

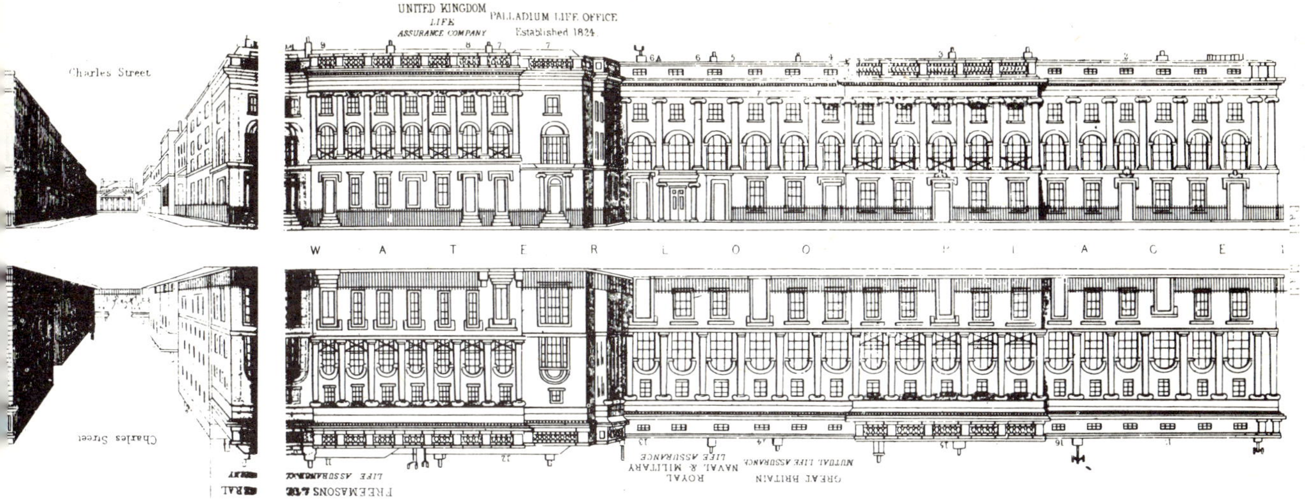


with an extra door onto the street. This seems to have been abandoned in favour of smart private residences but by 1848 there were several assurance offices established in the street.

Lower Regent Street proper began just above Charles Street, with Warren's Hotel on the west. Shortly after this view was published, the façade was altered: a double portico was added, the pediment removed and a third storey with segmental windows and a mansard attic storey added to increase the accommodation. Iron balconettes were installed on the Charles Street front.

Opposite was the Junior United Services Club, still using Smirke's original clubhouse built for the Senior Club, as altered by Burton in 1830. No. 3 was Hopkinson's Bank, and next door the commercial block, Nos. 5, 7 and 9, developed by John Howell, a silk mercer, who occupied first two houses and then the whole block for his business. Howell and James remained there as silk mercers and jewellers until the 1890s, and then rather curiously turned into estate agents in the first decade of this century. Opposite was Burton's Carlton Chambers—Nos. 4–12, part bachelor lodgings and part offices.

designed by Decimus Burton, replaced Mr Blicke's private house in 1838. It was destined to undergo several metamorphoses in the course of the nineteenth century. By the 1870s it had become an auctioneers; by the 1890s it was known as York House, and had become the home of the Junior Army and Navy Stores Ltd.

On the east side were Nos. 14 and 16, containing Nash's and Edwards's houses which were later to become the homes of various minor clubs. No. 22 was the shop of Elkington's the jewellers, from the 1840s until 1910.

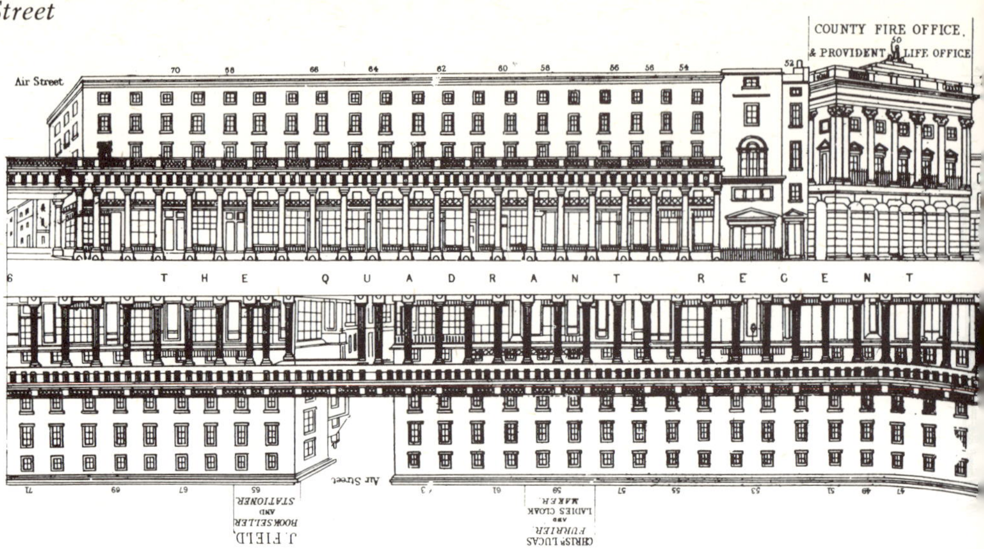


**Piccadilly Circus and part of the Quadrant**
This section shows Regent Circus South, today Piccadilly Circus, to the end of the Quadrant. There were a number of interesting shops in the Circus, not all of which are named in this edition. Several tradesmen held the Royal Warrant; Ponsonby & Son at No. 32, carvers and gilders to the Queen, and at No. 35 J. Read, instrument makers to the late King William IV, and to the East India Company.

There were already a number of travel firms established in the Circus, carrying on the tradition of the great Piccadilly coaching inns. There was a railway and coach office at No. 33 and the South Eastern Railway had an office at No. 40, having taken over the Bull and Mouth Coach Office. The whole of the north-western segment was then occupied by Hollidays

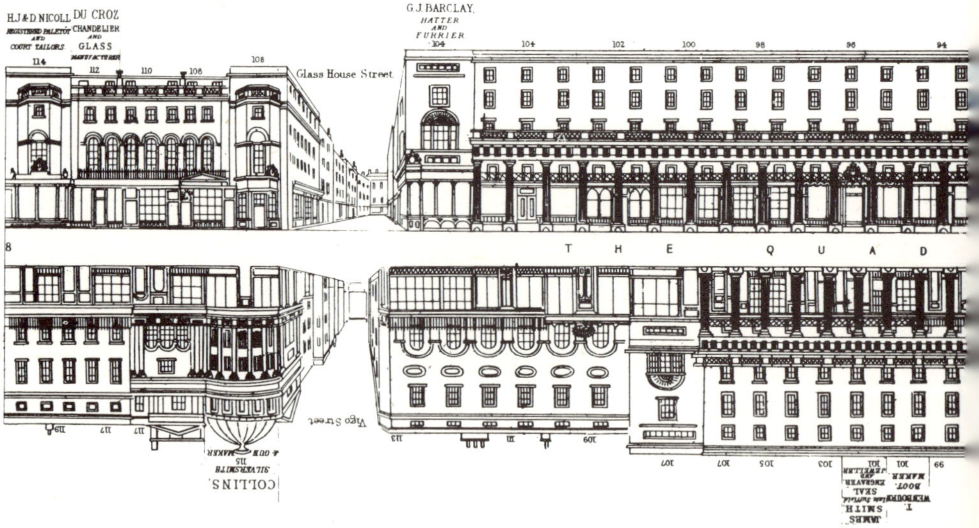


**Quadrant and part of Regent Street**
There were a number of billiard rooms in the Quadrant, of which Smith's, at No. 82, was well known for its pool games. Phillips, sharing No. 99 with a boot and shoe warehouse, later became the headquarters for an exclusive coterie of titled clubmen, which included Attenborough, 'King of Pawnbrokers'. In the lurid words of a Victorian journalist: 'No goat from an alien flock dared hope to browse on that jealously guarded pasture.'

A number of the shops had striking windows; there were at least two sculptors—Denman at No. 83, and Gaffin's Carrara Marble Works which remained at No. 63 until it was demolished in 1925.

No. 93 housed an unusual husband and wife team, Mrs Lipscombe, corset maker, and Lipscombe & Co.,

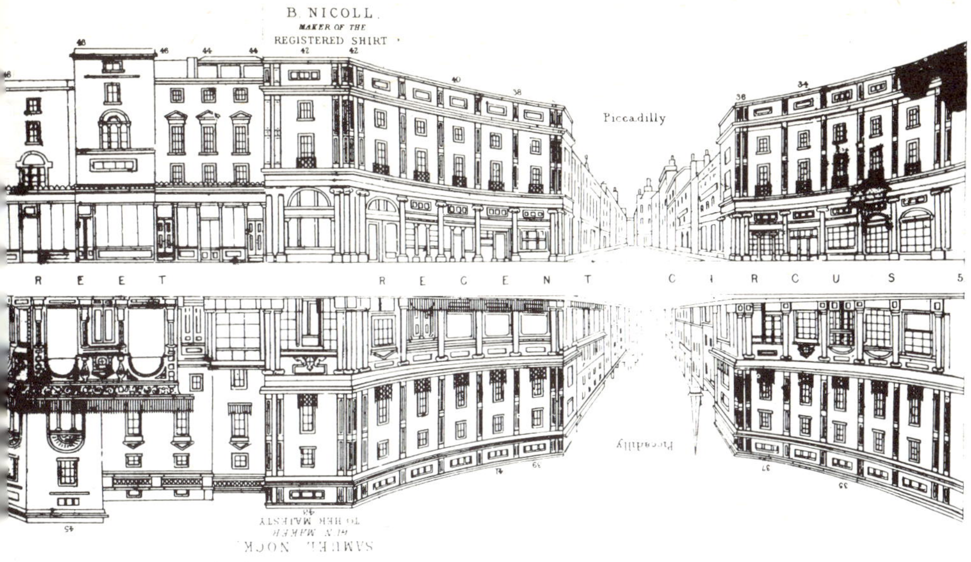


Universal Booking Office.

Swan and Edgar, linen-drapers, occupied Nos. 39–51, having expanded since 1838. They had already struck out in favour of shopkeepers' individuality by putting up an arresting new façade. In the Quadrant itself there were as yet few familiar establishments. The emphasis at this period was on a great variety of small shops providing an immense range of goods and services. It was mostly occupied by milliners, together with a number of hatters, hosiers, bonnet makers and shawl warehouses. It is interesting that they were all specialist shops of one sort or another, and usually not only salesmen but also craftsmen who made their own wares. The exceptions were warehousemen who, as their name implied, marketed other people's goods.

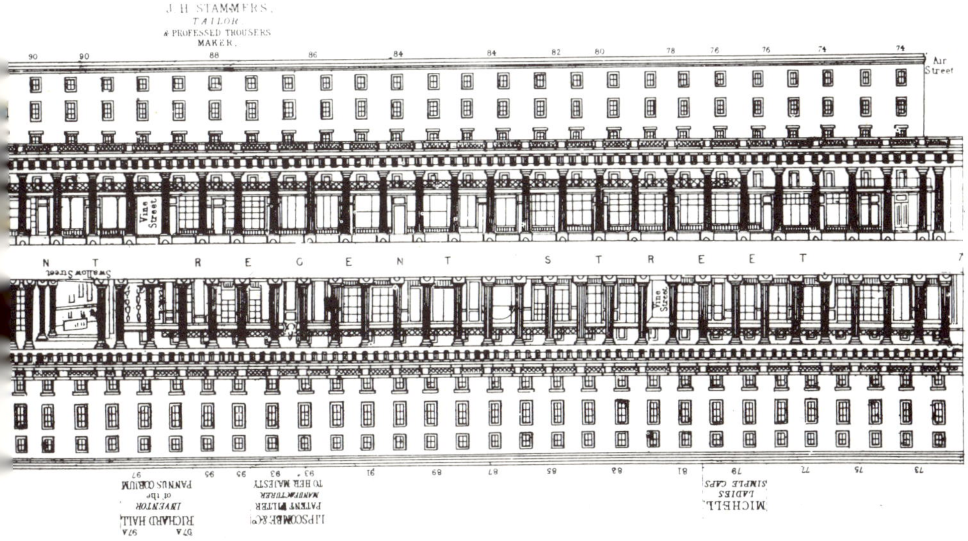


who sold water filters—very necessary with the doubtful Victorian water supply. Fifty years later Sala remembered the 'mimic and miniature version of the *Grandes Eaux* at Versailles' which demonstrated 'the astonishing machines for converting foul and muddy water, like gruel, thick and slab, into a sparkling, crystal stream'.

At No. 83 was W. Tucker, naturalist, in whose house Sala lodged with his mother. His home was full of specimens for stuffing, and his window full of Birds of Paradise, parrots and humming birds of gorgeous plumage.

At No. 60 was C. Barbe, artists' colourman, subsequently better known as Lechertier-Barbe, whose window boasted a macabre waxwork of a would-be assassin of King Louis Philippe, badly wounded by his own infernal machine.

**Regent Street: Beak Street to Leicester Street**
A lot of the façades seem to have been revised for this second edition of the Street View, and particularly interesting is the way in which the shop fronts have become more elaborate and more individualistic. The windows are still shown, however, as a mixture of small panes and the new-fangled plate glass.

Almost everything in this drawing was developed by James Burton, and though we do not know the name of the designer, it could possibly have been Decimus Burton, James's young architect son. The exception is the very distinguished block designed by Sir John Soane for Mr Robins (Nos. 156–170). It is unfortunately

**Regent Street: New Burlington Street to Conduit Street**
Starting on the east side, one of the most important façades was that of Archbishop Tenison's Chapel. This had stood there since 1702, but had suffered the indignity of being incorporated in the east side of the street. The new stone façade was designed by Charles Robert Cockerell. At No. 182 were the famous wine merchants Carbonell & Company. John Carbonell employed Robert Abraham, architect of the County Fire Office, to design this block—the centre house of which provided a home and office.

At No. 194 was H. Melton, hatter to the Prince Consort, one of whose masterpieces was painted by

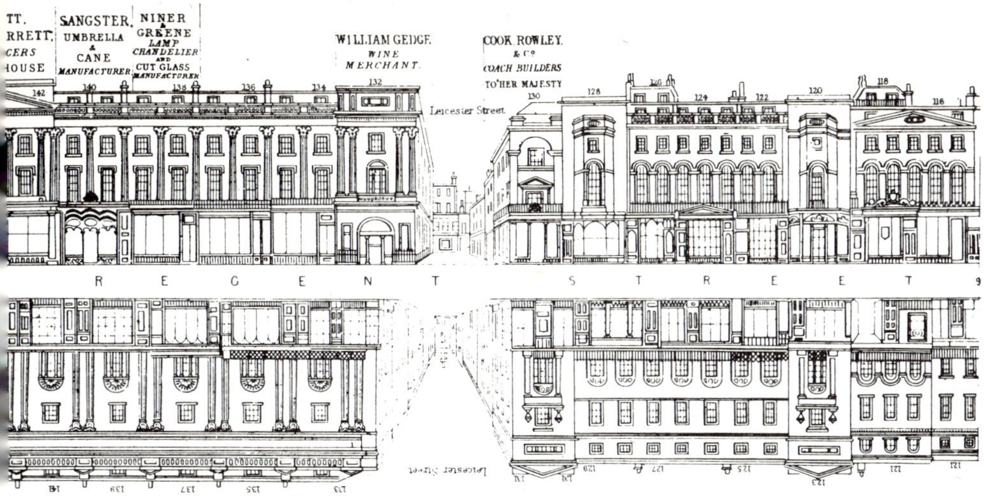


divided here in this view, and its original purity is already a little impaired by the curious shop windows which have sprouted at No. 170, the premises of Messrs Benhams, paperhangers.

Newman's Livery stables were at No. 121 on the west side and in the mews behind. Newman was the only surviving livery stable-keeper of Swallow Street, and he remained there as job master until the 1890s and the stables were then replaced by the New Gallery.

Miss Clarke at No. 154 is said to have made a fortune out of antique lace, and to have been buried in it.

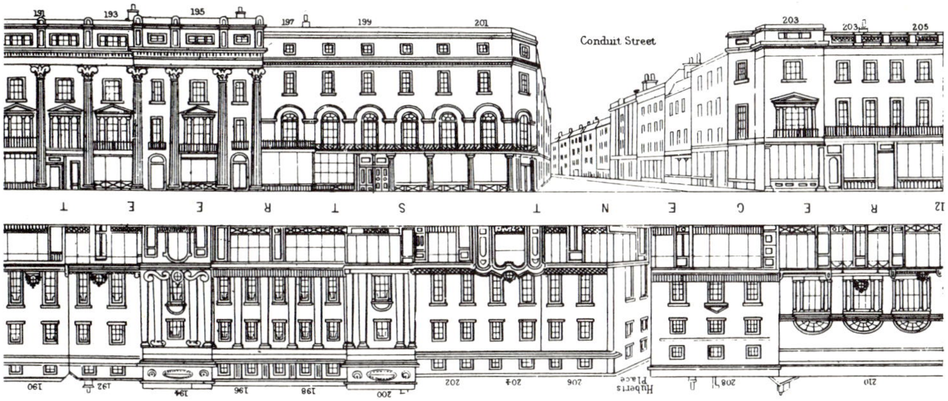


Landseer, along with the Prince's gloves and two of the Prince's favourite dogs. 'If Sir Edwin had only moved that hat two inches and a half to the right', he used to sigh, 'so as to exhibit the Royal Arms inside the crown, and the inscription 'H. Melton, Hatter to His Royal Highness the Prince Consort! . . .'

The very elaborate façade at No. 204 housed a series of goldsmiths. No. 210 was the purpose-built premises of Smith's the coachbuilders, designed by John White.

At 189 was a Post Office receiving house, forerunner of the Regent Street Post Office. No. 191 belonged to Ackermann, the well-known print publisher, and at No. 201 were the music publishers Cramer, Beale & Co.

**Regent Street: Conduit Street to Princes Street**
No. 218, east side, had been the original home of the confectioners Verreys, now at No. 229 across the street. It was now occupied by a number of businesses, including the Argyll billiard rooms, and Mayo & Co., manufacturers of mineral waters. Next door were Savory & Moore, originally established in 1826 and at No. 232 were Dickins, Smith and Stevens, founders of Dickins and Jones. Further north were a collection of furriers, including the Baffin's Bay Co., and the catholically named Russian & Canadian Fur Co., at No. 244. At No. 256–260 were Hodge and Lowman, linen-drapers. It was here that Mayhew's ratcatcher described catching some black Norwegian rats from which he bred a successful strain of fancy pied rats.

At Nos. 246–252 had been the Harmonic Institution, rebuilt by Nash in 1818 on the site of the Argyll Rooms. It was burnt down in 1830,

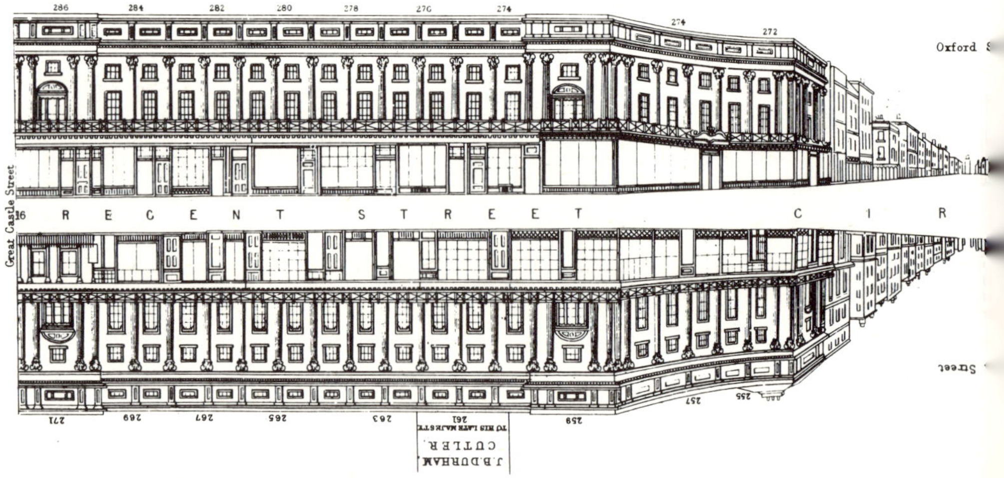


**Oxford Circus**
The whole of Regent Circus North was developed by Samuel Baxter, presumably to the design of Nash. In some ways the larger, more open, and slightly more ornate Corinthian pilasters make this northern Circus more splendid than the southern one, but it does not seem to be quite so

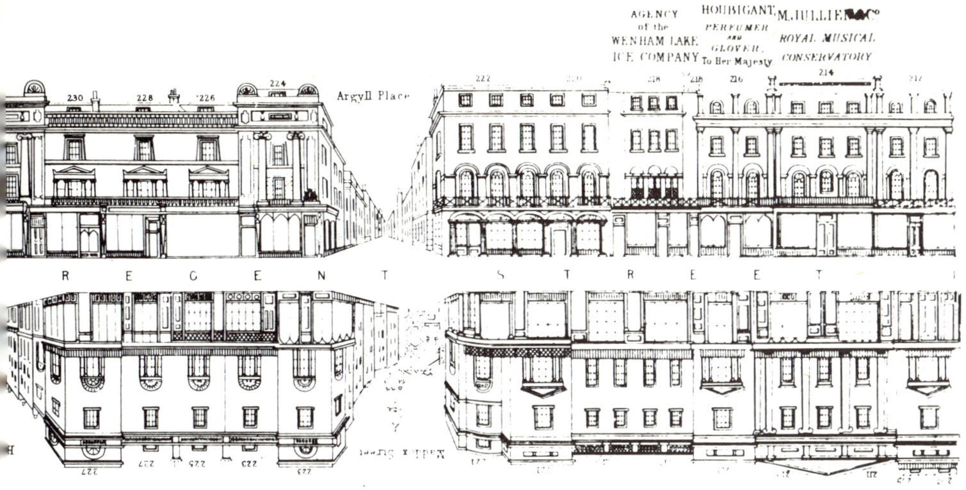


and reconstructed as shops. The curved façade of No. 246 formed an eye-catcher for the top end of the street as did No. 115 for the Quadrant. The block at Nos. 226–238 was built by Samuel Baxter but his architect is unknown.

The Hanover Chapel, designed by C. R. Cockerell and consecrated in 1825, was haunted by 'Italian image-boys'—lads who were sent out to sell plaster casts of medals and *alti-relievi* and plaster effigies of a variety of subjects—the Venus de Milo, Canova's Three Graces, the Dying Gladiator, Shakespeare, the Duke of Wellington, and Queen Victoria herself. The fashion for this brand of art died out as the century progressed, though followers of Sherlock Holmes will recall the story of the *Six Napoleons*.

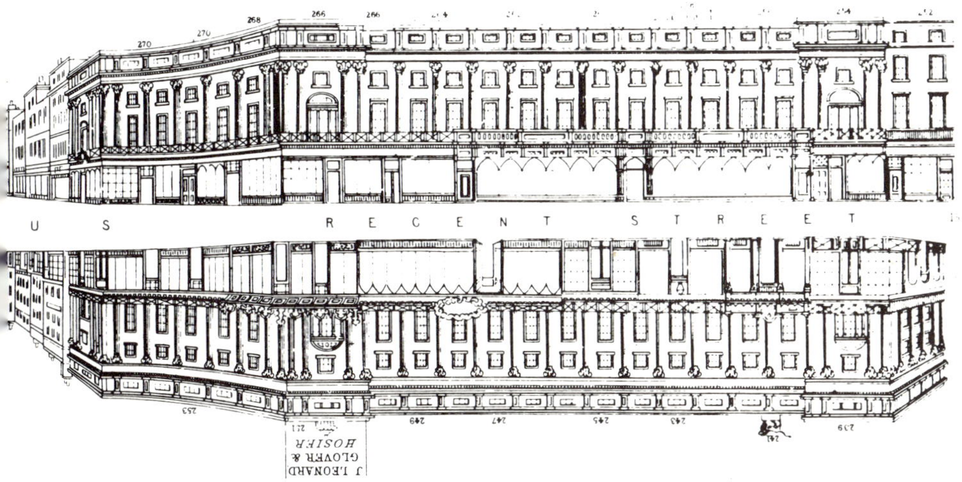


prosperous at this period. The changes in the shop fronts reveal where amalgamations had taken place. On the east side, Nos. 256–262 all belonged to Hodge and Lowman, while the north-eastern quadrant belonged to Messrs Williams & Company, linen-drapers.

The Circus is splendidly engraved, but few tradesmen seem to have paid for having their names inserted. W. C. Jay, mourning warehouseman, was already established at No. 247, forerunner of one of the most important emporia in Regent Street.

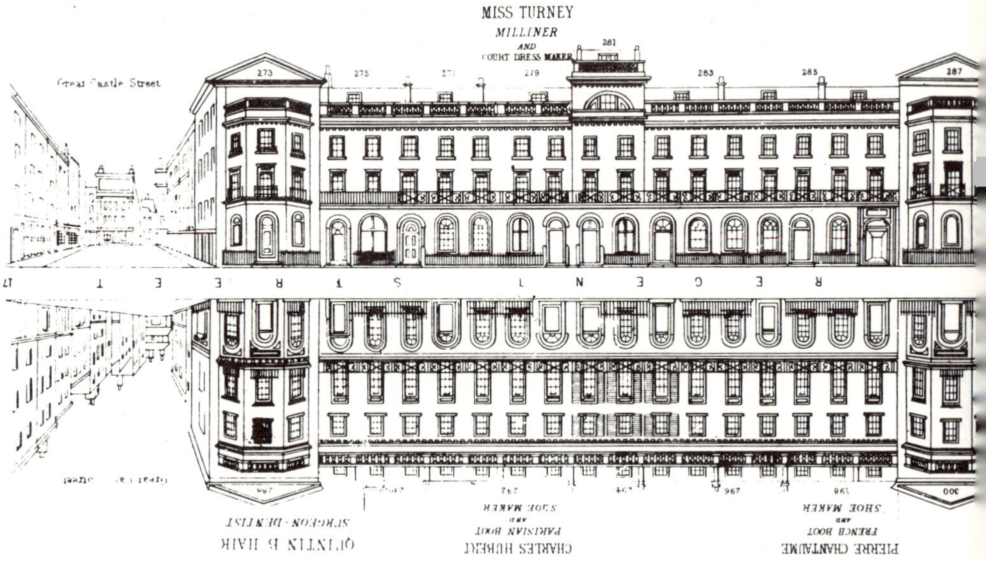


**Regent Street: Castle Street to Margaret Street**

Again, much of the area north of the Circus was developed by Baxter. He was responsible for the two balancing blocks immediately north of the Circus with their curious bays on the pedimented outside blocks. (Nos. 273–287 and 288–300).

This part of the Street changed a good deal in its early years. The block between Mortimer Street and Margaret Street originally consisted of two grand three-house blocks with a row of arcaded stable buildings between, Nos. 295–311 inclusive.

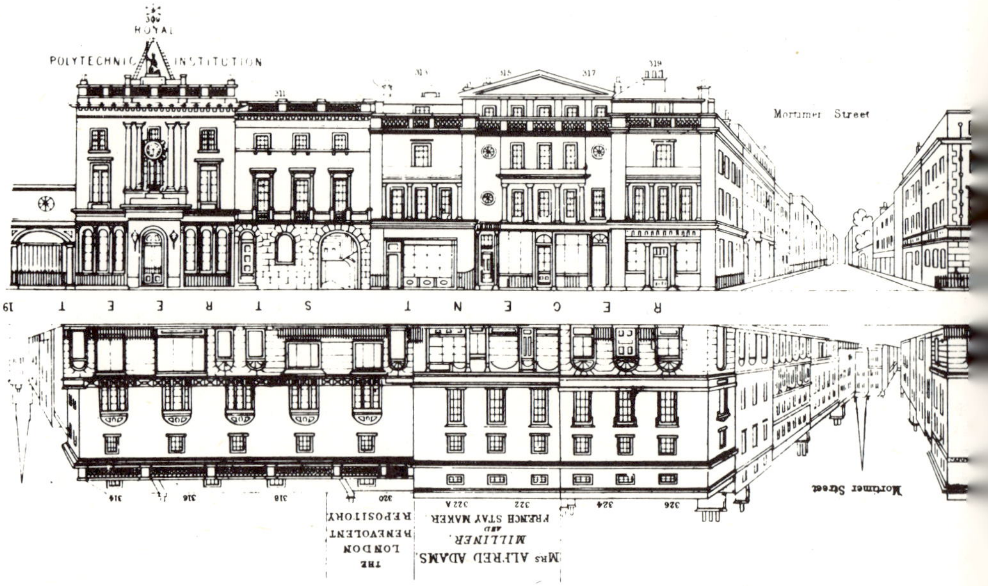

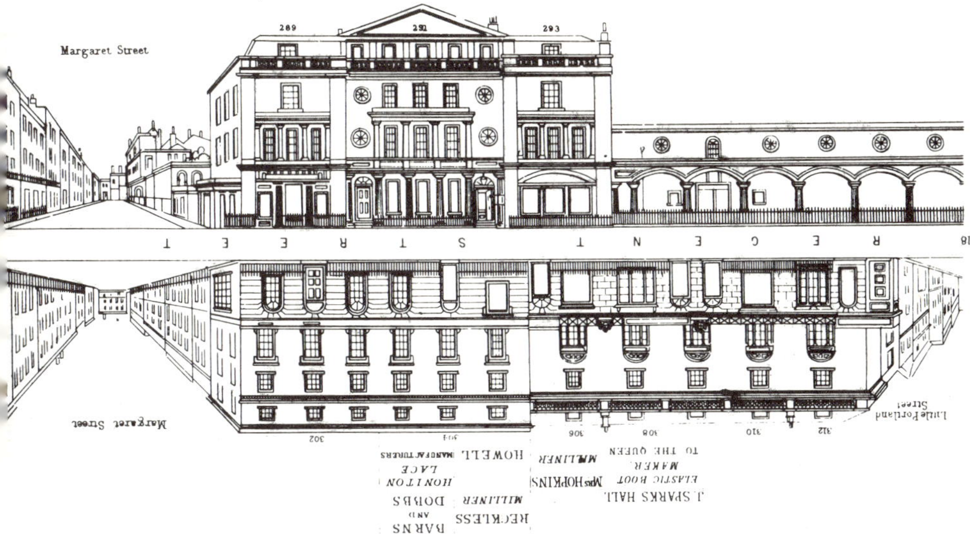


No. 309, later the Polytechnic, was built in the middle of the stable building, and, still later, Messrs Turner, veterinary surgeons, built themselves new premises at No. 311.

At the northern end of the west side were the gardens of Langham House, whose main frontage was northward to Portland Place.

On the east side next to the church originally stood the London Carriage Repository, an elegant low building shown on the earlier version of Tallis. By 1847, however, Mr Marks, the owner, had built the substantial block of four houses shown here.

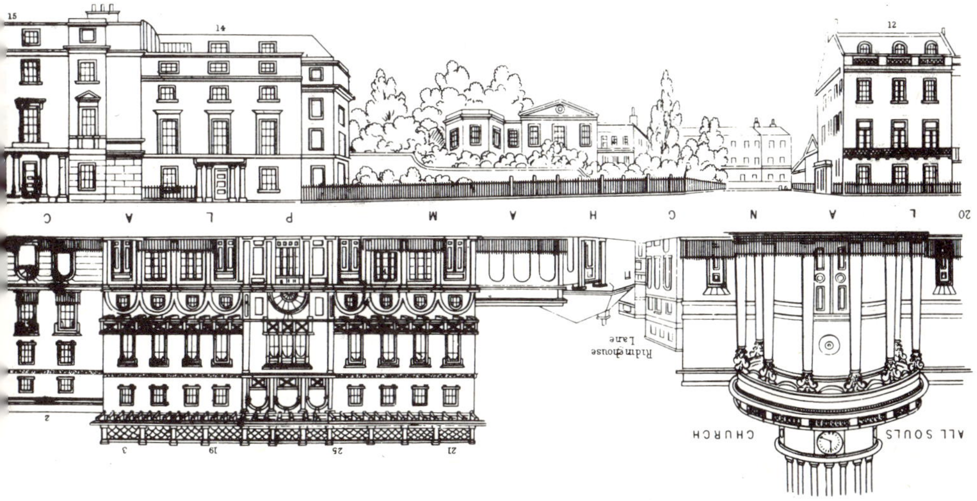

# III

# The only boulevard in London

J.A. DUNN
CO.
STERLING HOUSE
MUSIC ROLLS FOR ALL PIANO PLAYERS
STERLING
MUSIC ROLLS FOR ALL PIANO PLAYERS
J.A. DUNN & CO.
DUNN.
LADIES TAILOR &
SOUTHWOOD
96
SOUTHWOOD
98
94
LD5299

# Architectural changes in the later nineteenth century

'If you stroll down Regent Street, the Quadrant, and Waterloo Place, any fine afternoon,' wrote a somewhat chauvinist Londoner in 1843, 'you cannot fail to remark vast numbers of exotics in glossy black silk hats, with *moustaches* and whiskers to match, hard inexpressive coats, flash satin vests, unwhisperables plaited ridiculously over the hips, glazed leather boots, and a profusion of Birmingham jewellery and Bristol stones . . .'

These French *émigrés*, the writer went on, revealed their political opinions by their moustaches: Bonapartist, Legitimist or Jacobin—all could be recognised.

The French were only one foreign element in Regent Street: there were also a number of Italians and Germans, often associated with the Opera or the concert rooms. More foreigners lived in the streets off Golden Square than in Regent Street itself, particularly as the shops themselves expanded into the upper floors, but the Quadrant seems to have provided popular theatrical and operatic 'digs' in the mid-nineteenth century. The foreign impression was assiduously cultivated by the shopkeepers, since despite various attempts to promote home industry, fashion was largely dictated from Paris.

There were considerable changes in the new Regent Street but the inhabitants settled down and the street developed a personality and atmosphere which made it 'one of the most fashionable, the most interesting, and the most deservedly popular thoroughfares in the Metropolis'. It was regarded by visitors and Londoners alike as a splendid modern achievement, and an important element in any visit to London.

There were also important architectural changes, which affected the southern part of the street very considerably.

The first major change to take place in Regent Street was the removal in 1848 of the Quadrant arcades, 'always a favourite project of Mr Nash's, never a favourite one with the public'. They had been intended originally to provide a covered walk for the nobility and gentry on rainy days, and possibly they might have achieved this had they been extended further. In the event the colonnade was found to be a 'haunt for vice and immorality', and when the Commissioner canvassed the owners, most were in favour of demolition:

'I consider it (the Colonnade) to have been the cause of that part of Regent Street being so decidedly inferior, for business purposes and letting . . . the covered way is the cause of more vice being engendered than in any other street west of Temple Bar. In what other part of Regent Street will you find so many small and petty shops?'

Leverton had rejected the idea of colonnades round the Opera House on the grounds that they would be liable to abuses of this kind, but Nash had thought he could avoid some of the problems by making the columns round! It must also be said in his favour that the evidence does not suggest that the gambling and prostitution complained of disappeared with the colonnade. Only one lessee, a shopkeeper, supported Nash's view that the colonnades were valuable on wet days; more seemed to be irritated by the loss of light.

According to Sala, who as a child explored the roof leads above the colonnade, there was a lively and entertaining life amongst the lodgers, many of whom were both foreign and theatrical. Where else could have been seen Rossini sitting out with his wife and a magnificent macaw; or thirty-six Austrian child dancers rehearsed by their sergeant-major of a chorus-mistress and impresario; or indeed the tenor of the Italian Opera, with knife in hand, pursuing his wife in her nightdress? Other activities not perhaps envisaged by Nash, were the use of peashooters on cats and on other occupants of the balconies, and, requiring more skill, the removal of the hats from passers-by, by deft manipulation of a salmon-hook attached to a tandem-whip.

Some outside observers were against the removal of the colonnade which had indeed become one of London's great tourist attractions, and foreign prints of it were often captioned simply *'Ville de Londres!'* Despite such opposition the Commissioners, having polled their lessees in 1846, proceeded to commission James Pennethorne, the official architect, to remove the colonnades, and to restore the façades with an enriched string course under the second floor, new balconies for the first floor, and reorganised mezzanines. The colonnades

**Previous page** The Quadrant in 1912

**Below** The removal of the Quadrant colonnades in October 1848, from the *Illustrated London News*. In the words of Augustus Sala: 'Whatever could have possessed our Commissioners of Woods and Forests to allow those unrivalled arcades to be demolished!'
**Right** Regent Street, Glasshouse Street and Tichborne Street from the Quadrant about 1860, showing the effect of the removal of the colonnades.

were pulled down in the autumn of 1848, and the cast iron columns and other materials were sold at public auction. The *Builder* mourned their passing on November 4th, 1848:
'. . . the destruction is complete. One of the most striking features of modern London has been cut off its face, and a great public injury committed, to gratify a score of persons who fancy they will be individually benefitted by the removal of the colonnade.'

The shops were certainly lighter, but there seems little evidence for the improvement in public morals, and 'the moustached foreigners, together with some gaily-dressed company still naughtier', continued to prowl around the lower end of Regent Street.

**Right** Regent Street, Tichborne Street, and Regent Circus South in 1870, before the making of Shaftesbury Avenue.
**Left** No. 48 Regent Street, Glasshouse Street and the County Fire Office, from Swan and Edgar's, about 1880. The shops on the right were removed in 1885 for the making of Shaftesbury Avenue. Emary and Co. can be seen at No. 48.
**Below** Piccadilly Circus in 1880, after the creation of Shaftesbury Avenue, and the building of the London Pavilion.

More far-reaching changes were caused by another metropolitan improvement—the creation of Shaftesbury Avenue, and the demolition of part of Regent Circus South in 1885.

Like other schemes for improving London, this one was projected long before it was carried out. As early as 1838 a new street connecting the east end of Oxford Street directly with both Charing Cross and Piccadilly was suggested. Unfortunately it drove directly through some of the worst slums in the West End, and also involved over a mile of new streets. This made it an operation on the scale of Regent Street, without the benefit of Crown ownership of much of the land. The Metropolitan Board of Works, set up to carry out such improvements, began with those in the City and also with the relatively uncomplicated Thames Embankment, but by 1876 the increased traffic pressure generated by these made inevitable the creation of Charing Cross Road and Shaftesbury Avenue. The M.B.W. started operations, and though hardly a very efficient body, and one whose reputation for jobbery was unenviable, it was hamstrung by restrictions placed upon it by Parliament. One restriction—the necessity to rehouse the slum dwellers displaced by the scheme—had little effect on the planning of Piccadilly Circus; the other can probably be blamed for much of the resulting visual squalor of the area since. This was the paring down to a minimum the area allowed for compulsory purchase, which left the Board with no room for manoeuvre in re-planning the new open space. Nor was there enough profit from the new frontages on to Shaftesbury Avenue to pay for a good architectural solution to the Circus problem. Unfortunately it was perhaps the worst possible moment in the history of London's government to carry through such a scheme successfully – to make this point one needs only to contrast Shaftesbury Avenue with Regent Street, or with the later Kingsway, which displays that civic consciousness that was always such an influence in the early days of the London County Council.

The solution adopted was very simple – it was to carry the line of the existing King Street through the intervening blocks, and to sweep away altogether the north-eastern quadrant of Piccadilly Circus thus creating an amorphous open space. Instead of a real circus which contained the vistas from the streets of Piccadilly, Lower Regent Street, and the Quadrant so effectively (see page 33), what is now left is the statue of Eros and a number of traffic management schemes which are a visual acknowledgement of the uncertainty of Londoners about what to do with one of their most important open spaces.

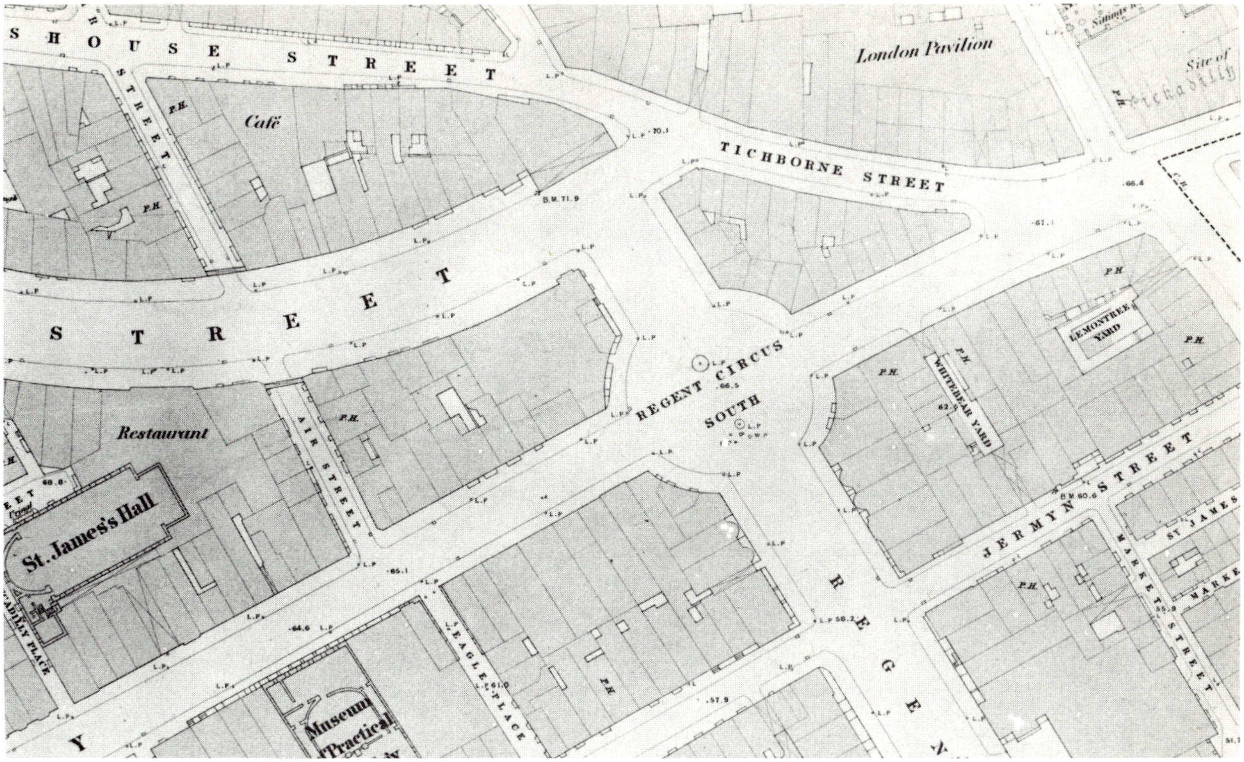
London Pavilion
Café
TICHBORNE STREET
REGENT CIRCUS SOUTH
Restaurant
AIR STREET
St. James's Hall
LEMONTREE YARD
WHITEBEAR YARD
JERMYN STREET
EAGLE PLACE
Museum

New Gallery
DENMAN STREET
Café Monico
Royal Trocadero Music Hall
GLASSHOUSE STREET
Café Royal
London Pavilion Music Hall
VIGO STREET
Royal London Yacht Club
Royal Geographical Society
REGENT STREET
Shaftesbury Memorial
Lavatory
PICCADILLY CIRCUS
Criterion Theatre
SACKVILLE STREET
SWALLOW STREET
Police Station
VINE STREET
St. James's Hall
Restaurant
JERMYN STREET
Bank
Museum of Practical Geology
BURLINGTON HOUSE
Royal Society
Geological Society
The Mission
Fire Alarm
Drinking Fountain
Vestry Hall
St. James's Church Seats for 1500
Prince's Hall
Junior Army & Navy Stores
Raleigh Club
APPLE TREE YARD

Typical of the lack of coordination between the relevant authorities was the disagreement about the building of an underground lavatory below the smaller piece of land left over by the scheme. The Board felt that such a use would be improper, but the Vestry of St James's saw it as a necessary public utility. The Board absolutely forbade any such use, then discovered that by law the land in question had to be transferred to the Vestry. It was possibly this fiasco as well as the increasing rumbling about the corruption of the Board, that decided the Board, in 1887, to abandon two further schemes. One of these was a scheme to build a small low group of shops on the larger island. Their second thoughts on the subject were for a pair of archways on the site of the vanished north-east segment through which the traffic from Shaftesbury Avenue would have passed. In the event they did nothing, leaving a formless open space which has caused endless argument ever since, much of which will be dealt with later on, (see page 115). The final row was about the statue of Eros, in memory of the great Earl of Shaftesbury,

Three interesting buildings were added to Piccadilly Circus at this time, which would not have effected Regent Street earlier, but which were thrown into juxtaposition by the new 'Circus'.

The first was the Criterion Restaurant on the south side, which replaced the famous White Bear Inn, one of the great coaching inns of London. By the mid-nineteenth century the inn had been 'taken over by sporting characters', though Webb's hotel next door was still respectable. On the eastern part of the site was the 'Pic', the 'haunt of pickpockets, bullies and "soiled doves" of a very mediocre class, a dancing saloon of a decidedly inferior class, where anybody entering (except perhaps the Archangel Gabriel) was bound to have a row. Hat-smashing . . . was the preliminary to a scrimmage . . .'

The Criterion was built by the famous catering firm of Spiers and Pond in 1871, to the designs of Thomas Verity (1837–1891). It was originally

**Above** Shaftesbury Avenue and Piccadilly Circus about 1912 showing the Café Monico and the London Pavilion.

**Left** Piccadilly Circus in 1909 showing the effect of the removal of the north-eastern quadrant.

**Left** Interior of the new Café Monico about 1914 showing the lavish interior decoration. The café was built in 1888–9 to the designs of Messrs Christopher and White.
**Below** Regent Circus South in 1910 dwarfed by the Criterion. The traditional connection with travel lasted in this part of Piccadilly for one hundred years, extending from the stage-coach to the aeroplane.
**Right** Piccadilly Circus in 1900 with the London Pavilion and the Piccadilly Restaurant on the left and the Criterion Theatre and Restaurant on the right. In the centre can be seen the Shaftesbury Memorial Fountain, better known as Eros, designed by the sculptor Alfred Gilbert as a national memorial to the philanthropist Lord Shaftesbury (1801–1885). Its siting and design caused more trouble than usual for public testimonials. Gilbert described the Piccadilly Circus site as 'a distorted isochromal triangle, square to nothing of its surroundings – an impossible site . . . upon which to place

any outcome of the human brain, except possibly an underground lavatory!' The attempt to provide an ornamental fountain combined with 'refreshment to thirsty man and beast' was impossible, and presented an irresistible challenge to hooliganism. It was unveiled in June 1892.

designed as a tavern with a number of large rooms for entertainments, but before it was completed the owners applied for permission to turn the basement concert hall into a theatre. The building is interesting for a number of reasons—it is one of the first theatres built in a basement, possible only because of the development of modern services such as lifts and mechanical ventilation. It is also one of the first buildings to use ornamental tilework as the chief decoration. This was to become a major decorative form in late Victorian and Edwardian London, both internally and externally, and was used on Delissa Joseph's Tube Station of 1903, next door to the Criterion.

The new London Pavilion was built on a curious triangular site at the south-west corner of the new Circus. The original London Pavilion had been demolished for the making of Shaftesbury Avenue, and by a curious and discreditable series of transactions, the theatre and subsequently the building lease for the new one, had been acquired by a music-hall proprietor, R. E. Villiers. The original character of London music-halls was shown in the way in which the theatre was originally furnished with boxes in the dress circle, open seats in the gallery, and marble-topped tables with banquettes in the pit.

The Café Monico at No. 15 Tichborne Street was a humble restaurant run by the Monico brothers, former partners of the Gatti family in their confectionery and ice business in the Strand. With the creation of Piccadilly Circus, No. 15 Tichborne Street became No. 46 Regent Street, and the brothers extended their premises into Shaftesbury Avenue.

The rebuilding of Piccadilly Circus stimulated change in the Haymarket. This street had had a

rather chequered history since the creation of Regent Street. Certain parts of the street, like the two theatres, had been drawn into the scheme but the top end had been virtually untouched. The hay and straw market had been removed to Cumberland Market in 1830.

The Haymarket seems to have become the centre of West End night life in the 1860s—one writer described it as blazing with light until daybreak, from various restaurants and taverns. Not all of these were reputable, and one at least was so ruinous that it literally fell down one night engulfing the proprietor, who had rushed back into the collapsing building to save his cashbox. A lot of the glory of the Haymarket departed with the fire at the Opera House in 1867, which left the theatre burnt out. It did not reopen until 1875, and even then it never regained its old popularity or its standing as one of London's three leading theatres.

The effect of the rebuilding of Piccadilly Circus combined with the loss of the Opera House was severe. Night-life continued in the Haymarket, but it was no longer fashionable:

'The Haymarket,' wrote a contemporary, 'from the exalted position of the centre of the surging mass of nocturnal corruption has descended to the status of a dimly-lighted thoroughfare, with here and there an unlicensed Italian restaurant and a sprinkling of second class pot-houses.'

It took two of the greatest figures in late Victorian London to restore the standing of the Haymarket. Prolonged negotiations for rebuilding on the Opera House site took place between 1889 and 1895, and finally a scheme for building both a new theatre and an hotel on the site was agreed. These were designed by C. J. Phipps (1835–1897), the leading theatre architect of his day.

Herbert Beerbohm Tree, the great actor-manager, elder brother of Max Beerbohm, and one of the best known figures of the Edwardian stage, was then manager at the Haymarket Theatre. He moved across the road to Her Majesty's, and not only managed but lived in the theatre until his death in 1917. His famous series of productions begun in 1897 restored the reputation of the theatre.

The Carlton Hotel, on the Pall Mall front of the Opera site, was taken by a man equally famous as a hotelier, César Ritz. Ritz had started his career working at the Savoy Hotel, but this had ended in a dramatic row. He took the new hotel, completed internally and decorated by his architect, Méwès. It opened in 1899 and boasted all the elements from which he had created the 'Ritz' style—marvellous French cooking, very high standards of service, distinguished décor, and above all his famous palms, on which the Prince of Wales is said to have complimented him.

These new theatres and restaurants, with their variety of dining rooms, were a sign of the greater affluence and the wider choice in entertainment offered by London to its inhabitants. One has only to look at the large number of theatres built and rebuilt in the period, and the restaurants and hotel dining rooms developed to cater for the much larger number of people who could afford to eat out, to appreciate the gaiety and liveliness of late Victorian and Edwardian London.

**Left** Opera House, Haymarket, under demolition in 1892. Negotiations for its redevelopment were prolonged, and Her Majesty's Theatre at the top end of the site was not completed and opened until 1897, and the Carlton Hotel at the southern end until 1899.
**Right** The Carlton Hotel and Her Majesty's Theatre in 1957.
**Below** The Haymarket, looking north, about 1905, showing the Theatre Royal on the right, and Her Majesty's, managed by Herbert Beerbohm Tree, on the left. There was a fierce rivalry between the two theatres.

## An avenue of superfluities . . .'

Most of the changes that took place in Regent Street after Nash's time were changes in its character rather than its architecture. Augustus Sala called it 'the most fashionable street in the world' in 1859, remarking on the subtle changes that had taken place:

'There was a dash of utilitarianism mingled with the slightly bohemian tinge of my Regent Street of twenty years ago; there were bakers' shops, stationers, and opticians, who had models of steam-engines in their windows. There was a grocer not above selling orange marmalade, brown sugar, and Durham mustard; . . . but I find the shop now expanded into a magnificent emporium, where are sold wines, and spirits, sweetmeats and preserves, liqueurs and condiments, Bayonne ham, Narbonne honey, Bologna sausages, Russian caviare, Iceland moss, clotted cream, and *terrines* of *pâté de foie gras* . . . Fancy watchmakers, haberdashers, and photographers; fancy stationers, fancy hosiers, and fancy staymakers; music shops, shawl shops, jewellers, French glove shops, perfumery and point lace shops, confectioners, and milliners . . .'

As well as the movement towards 'superfluities' there was a definite movement towards larger units spreading over three or more shops. These were often widely separated, and quite often housed distinct departments. Thus even in 1910 Peter Robinson, who occupied Nos. 252–264 at Oxford Circus, advertised No. 256 as their mourning warehouse, while Messrs Liberty's, though pursuing a policy of consolidation, had departments scattered up and down the east side. Some firms found this split personality profitable, like the milliners, Louise and Co., who had a useful connection with famous actresses like Sarah Bernhardt who were persuaded to wear their hats on stage. Their Regent Street shop, Maison Lewis, as they explained to the Crown Estate, was 'supported by the Crowned Heads of Europe and the English Aristocracy, while Louise and Co. is conducted as an ordinary English Millinery Business.' This seems to deserve the dry comment of a contemporary Crown Commissioner: 'You couldn't expect a Crowned head or the wife of a backwoods peer to shop in the same building with the ordinary gentlewoman.'

On the whole, however, consolidation was the object, and this increase in the size of businesses with every department under the same roof was the obvious trend. Even when large stores like Swan and Edgar continued to call themselves 'silk mercers' they were offering in addition a wide range of other goods.

Fashion was always Regent Street's main business, but other activities were carried on. The Quadrant had a strong artistic flavour, and Edward Gaffin's sculptor's business at No. 63 was a landmark from 1825 until 1925.

There were some half-dozen artists there in the 1840s, and of course other artistic establishments like Lechertier-Barbe, the colourmen, and the well known establishment of Rudolph Ackermann junior at No. 191, (page 51). He had his Eclipse Gallery, but there were other exhibition galleries in the Street. At No. 209 there was the Cosmorama exhibition in the early days, later Cramer's pianoforte gallery, while, lower down, the New Gallery at No. 121 was first an exhibition gallery and later an early cinema.

The artists were supplemented by photographers in the 1860s and particularly in the 1870s when there were thirty of various sorts—photographic artists, photographic miniature painters, and the London School of Photography (Saml. Prout Newcombe) at No. 174. The most famous was the London Stereoscopic Company which occupied Nos. 106–110 in the 1890s, whose 'great long double window' was recorded by Max Beerbohm. Kodak contributed one of the most interesting shop interiors.

**Top** The London Stereoscopic Company's premises at Nos. 106–110, in 1910. They were one of the best known of Regent Street's many photographic firms, established in the 1860s. Portraits of their better known sitters were displayed in the windows. Max Beerbohm recalled inspecting the windows at the age of 11: 'It was the London Stereoscopic Company that first opened my eyes to the fact that Churchill and Gladstone, Northcote and Harcourt, Chamberlain, Hartington and all those others were actual, mortal, modern men . . . The place of honour was accorded of course to members of the Royal Family. By precedence over Archbishops and Bishops, Generals, Admirals, Poets, Actors and Actresses, was taken by the Statesmen. They were not perhaps Gods, but they certainly were Titans, in the public eye. And here they all were in *my* eye, tailored and hosiered as men . . .'

**Centre** Photographic Exhibition at the New Gallery, 1897. The New Gallery was built during the 1880s on the former site of Newman's stables at 121 Regent Street. It became the New Gallery Cinema with the advent of films. The influence of George Walton, one of Kodak's chief designers of shop fascias and interiors, can be seen in the stencilling on the walls. (See also page 84)

**Bottom** Oxford Circus, Oxford Street, in 1910. Louise and Company were well-known milliners. They had two shops, both, they maintained, necessary for carrying on their business.

Perhaps the best known, though the least fashionable, artists in the street were the church glass painters Clayton and Bell, who occupied a former horse infirmary at No. 311 from about 1860 until they were displaced by the rebuilt Polytechnic.

There were a number of publishers and booksellers and stationers, not all of the fancy variety, if one recalls the sad story of Mr Fraser at No. 215. He published his own conservative magazine, which numbered among its contributors Harrison Ainsworth, Southey, Coleridge, and Dr Maginn. The last contributed an anonymous and vicious review of a novel by a Liberal Member of Parliament, Grantley Berkeley, who thought that the review had overstepped the bounds normally expected of a politically opposed reviewer. He went round to Fraser's shop in Regent Street and horsewhipped the poor editor to a 'mummy'. The unfortunate Fraser took his noble assailant to court and got a 'verdict and damages', but is said never to have recovered from the beating. Sala claims the story is an argument for the signed review—it also suggests that literary life at least has become less violent in the last 100 years!

There was a certain degree of violence in the life of the musical artistes who frequented Regent Street. However, by all accounts it seems to have been domestic in nature and to have taken place in the hotels and lodging houses of Golden Square and Soho where they lived, rather than in the shops in Regent Street which sold musical instruments or published music. The musical tradition was strong —it began with the Harmonic Institution at the top of the street, and continued with St George's Hall in Langham Place, and the famous concert rooms of the St James's Hall, opened in 1858.

The St James's Hall was promoted by, amongst others, the music publishers, William Chappell and T. F. Beale, who were inspired by 'the growing taste for Musical Performances of a high order, and upon an extensive scale'. This taste had led to the building of halls in Liverpool and elsewhere, though not yet in the metropolis. The Hall occupied the area immediately north of No. 28 Piccadilly, and stretched across to Nos. 69, 71 and 73, in the Quadrant. Owen Jones (1809–1874), who had decorated the interior of the Crystal Palace, was the architect. The large concert hall was galleried, had a great organ, and was decorated in the 'Florentine' style, with colour taken from the great Moorish palace of the Alhambra. The Piccadilly front was in a striking Gothic, but of course the elaborate complex of two restaurants and three halls was hidden discreetly behind Nash's Quadrant. The Hall kept its pre-eminence until challenged by the building of the Queen's Hall, in Langham Place, in 1891–3, and the Wigmore Hall, opened in 1901. This challenge, combined with the demands of the newly formed L.C.C.'s Fire Regulations, sounded the death-knell of the old St James's, whose replacement by the Piccadilly Hotel started a ten-year row between the Crown and their shopkeeper tenants in the Quadrant.

**Above** George Walton's decorated hoarding outside Kodak's new shop at Nos. 171–173. The new premises were opened in 1899 and much admired by the architectural press. George Walton (1867–1933) was a talented Glaswegian interior decorator who had worked with C.R. Macintosh, and who pioneered the idea of decorated hoardings. He did a great deal of work for Kodak's. His light airy interiors reflect the influence not only of Macintosh, but also of Whistler, and his painter brother E.A. Walton.

Plan of the New Street as published in 1813, showing the property belonging to the Crown, coloured blue and that which would have to be compulsorily purchased, coloured red.
*Plate IX*

*'Nashional Taste'*, a cartoon published in April 1824, after a Parliamentary debate in which the church was criticised. Nash is said to have joked to his assistants: "See, gentlemen, how criticism has exalted me!"
*Plate VIII*

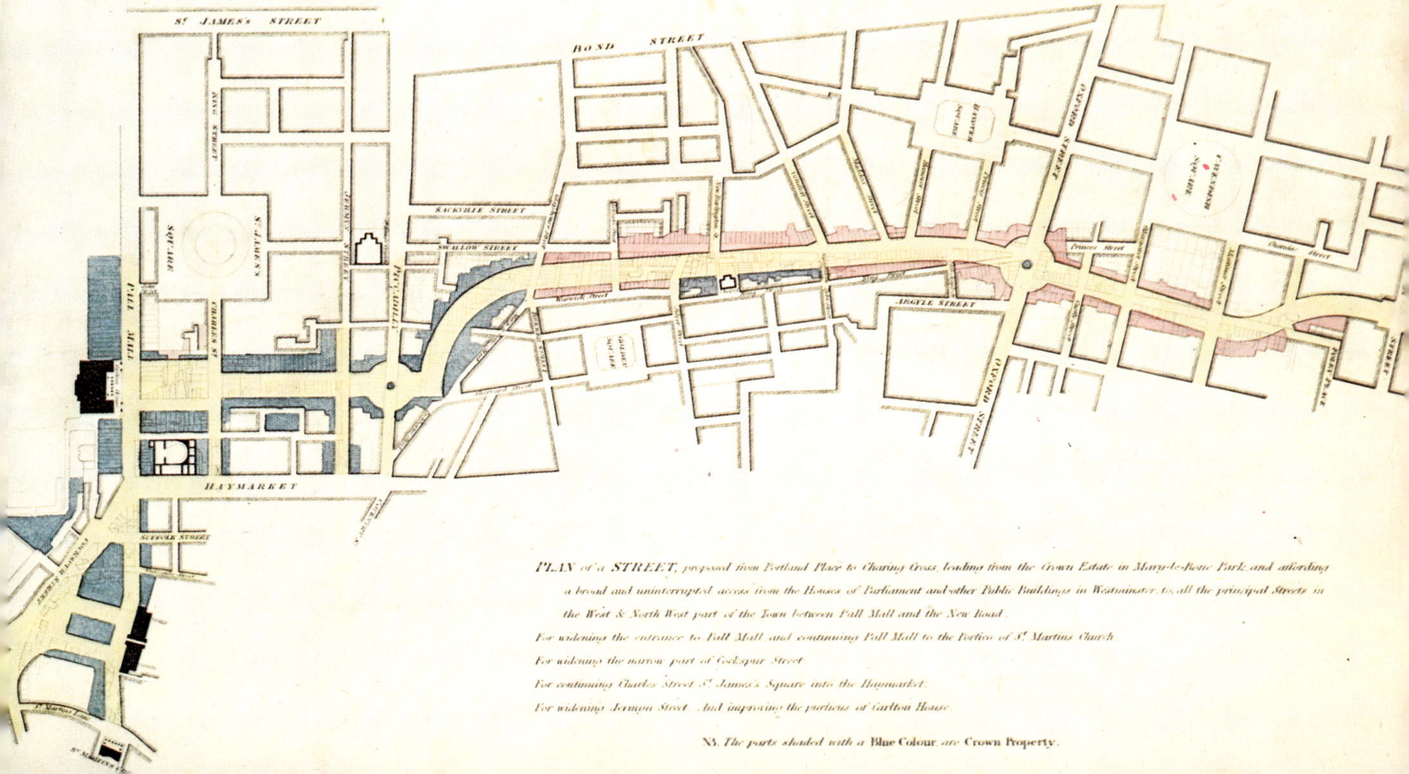

View from the Regent Circus, Piccadilly, looking south to Carlton House, in 1822. *Plate X*

HILL
HILL & Co
TAILOR & MILITARY WAREHOUSE

Waterloo Place with the Duke of York's Column, and Carlton House Terrace behind, 1831. *Plate XI*

Regent Street looking south from the Hanover Chapel in 1842, from T. S. Boys 'Orginal views of London as it is'. *Plate XII*

**Above** St James's Hall in 1858.
**Right** St George's Hall, Langham Place, opened in 1865.

But the St James's Hall left a musical tradition behind, and amongst the tenants in Regent Street in 1910 were the London Symphony Orchestra, who had their office at No. 61, and a number of concert agents. There was also a long tradition of musical instrument manufacturers. In the early days these included a flute maker, and Frederick Oetzman, pianoforte maker, at No. 151, and later Sir Herbert Marshall, pianoforte importers and manufacturers, at Regent House. Newfangled means of reproduction were not ignored: the Orchestrelle Company was established at No. 225 in the 1890s, and Pathé Frères, phonograph manufacturers, opened a London office at No. 64 in the next decade.

There were a number of theatrical agents who moved in after 1900, mostly, one suspects, to the

**Below** The Langham Hotel in 1910.
**Right** The vestibule of the Langham Hotel in the 1890s.

upper floors which had been occupied as theatrical 'digs', like those over 'a Scotch jeweller' at No. 221, occupied in 1870 by Joseph Kitchingman, proprietor of performing fleas.

There were other non-theatrical lodgers in Regent Street. Dickens, who knew the area well, and who used Golden Square as the home of Nicholas Nickleby, contrasted this with Lord Frederick Verisopht's 'handsome suite of private apartments in Regent Street'.

Langham Place saw a number of changes in the second half of the century, the most important being the building of the Langham Hotel on the site of Langham House and its extensive garden, in 1864–5.

This was designed by Murray and Giles, and the interior decoration was by Owen Jones. No expense was spared to make this not only one of the largest but one of the most up-to-date hotels in London. It had eight floors, two of which were service basements, and the total height of the building was 156 feet. It contained over 600 rooms, over thirty of which were suites with their own bathrooms, dressing-rooms and so forth, some 300 bedrooms in all, a large number of public rooms, including both a *salle-à-manger* and the more traditional coffee room, ladies' drawing rooms, billiard rooms and a number of committee rooms. Altogether it was enormous, one of the new generation of purpose-built luxury hotels which were a feature of mid-Victorian London. It was equipped with its own artesian well to supply a generous allowance of bathrooms and water-closets, as well as a private laundry, and boasted both passenger and service lifts.

The Prince of Wales paid a visit in June 1865, before its public opening, and this set the tone for the hotel which was both fashionable, without being fast, and successful. It was kept up to date, being refurbished in the 1890s, when the management set out their policy in a guide issued to visitors to London:

'The Executive has striven to introduce into the management the best points of the three systems—English, French and American—the object being to combine the comfort and discipline of the first with the elegance of the second and the organisation of the third. In the dining-hall the visitor can regale himself English fashion, take his seat at a well-furnished *table d'hôte*, or if aesthetic in his proclivities, dine *à la carte* in the latest French mode.'

The St George's Hall was opened in the same year as the hotel, on the other side of Langham Place, to meet the same demand for concert halls as the St James's Hall. Thirty years later, the Queen's Hall was built next door by the entrepreneur and businessman, Francis Mackenzie Ravenscroft, to the design of T. E. Knightley (1823–1905) and C. J. Phipps.

At No. 309 was the Royal Polytechnic Institution, first established in 1834 as a more scientific form of the exhibition hall so beloved of the inquiring Victorian visitor. In 1882 it was taken over by Quintin Hogg, who had started a night school for working lads in York Place off the Strand in 1865. This had proved so successful that he was forced to move to larger premises. The Polytechnic became a model for technical education, both in England and elsewhere.

QUEEN'S HALL
BOX OFFICE

QUEEN'S
HALL
PROMENADE
CONCERTS
QUINTIN
HOGG
ERECTED
BY THE MEMBERS
OF THE
POLYTECHNIC
TO THE
FOUNDER
FOREIGN
LANGHAM
PLACE
TEAS
PALMIST
LUNCHEONS

**Top left** The exterior of the Queen's Hall, Langham Place, in 1894.
**Bottom left** Langham Place and Upper Regent Street in 1910, before rebuilding, with the memorial to Quintin Hogg (1845–1903).
**Top right** The demolition of the Regent Street Polytechnic at Nos. 307–311 in Upper Regent Street in 1910. The old Polytechnic Institution had been bought by Quintin Hogg in 1882, to provide a home for a night-school for working lads, which he founded in York Place, Strand, in 1865. The Regent Street Polytechnic became the pioneer institution for technical education, both in full-time education and in evening classes. When rebuilding was undertaken there was a programme of 600 evening classes a week, and thirteen day schools. The cost of the new buildings was estimated at over one quarter of a million pounds.
**Bottom right** The interior of the Queen's Hall, the original home of the Promenade Concerts, in 1894. As in his Birbeck Bank in High Holborn for the same patron, Knightley is said to have chosen the colours for the interior with great care – grey of the shade of the belly of a London mouse, relieved with strawberry. More important perhaps were the acoustics, which were excellent. The Queen's Hall was managed by Robert Newman (1858–1926) who was responsible for the promotion of the Promenade Concerts from 1895, under the conductor Henry Wood. The Queen's Hall became London's leading concert hall after the demolition of the St James's Hall in 1905. It was burnt out in 1941, and the St George's Hotel now stands on the site.

In the nineteenth century, as today, Soho was very much the home of foreign restaurants, and for its first three decades Regent Street seems to have been catered for by these. The White Horse Tavern was at No. 169, but by 1870 this had become a wine merchant's shop, not perhaps any loss to the smart customers in the street, since public houses were on the whole the province of artisans and other working men. Confectioners were, however, different and Charles Verrey, an early resident at No. 231, who established his first shop at No. 218, had an instant success. His excellent ices were sold by his daughter Fanny, who seems to have managed to attract a number of aristocratic admirers whilst remaining faithful to a Swiss pastor in her native Lucerne. By 1848 the shop was established at No. 229, where it remained as a confectioner and café restaurant. Sherlock Holmes, when wanting something a little more special than Mrs Hudson's cooking, used to send to a confectioner's, and this was obviously a regular service. Verrey's became one of the leading restaurants of Edwardian London, recommended by Baedeker for its 'French cuisine (bouillabaise to order)'.

Reasonably priced food for the average mid-Victorian seems to have been provided by 'ham and beef' shops, presumably the equivalent of our modern delicatessen, and even in 1905 Baedeker could recommend the London pastry-cook for luncheon or dinner. Continental delicacies could be bought in Regent Street at Hermann Appenrodt's establishment near Oxford Circus at the same period, clearly the spiritual successor of Sala's grocer, while the Gambrinus restaurant in the Quadrant also catered for the large German community. By 1905, too, it was possible for the busy woman shopper to eat in the restaurants provided by her favourite department store, among them Swan and Edgar. Tea shops and cafés abounded in Edwardian London. J. Lyons opened a café at No. 168 in the 1890s, in the heart of Messrs Robinson and Cleaver's linen warehouse, while the Aerated Bread Company was established at No. 326, and No. 77, near St James's Hall.

**Far left** Verrey's Restaurant on the corner of Hanover Street in 1910.
**Left** The interior of Verrey's Restaurant in 1905.
**Above** West side of Regent Street, southward from Heddon Street to Vigo Street and the Quadrant, in 1912.

**Above** No. 8 Air Street as rebuilt by Daniel Nichols in 1870 to the design of Arthur Cates.

The most famous restaurant in Regent Street, if not in all Edwardian London, was the Café Royal, which had opened at Nos. 15–19 Glasshouse Street in 1865. The founder was a French *émigré*, Daniel Nicolas Thevenon, who found it more discreet to start business in London as Daniel Nichols. It is said that the Imperial 'N' surrounded with the Imperial laurel wreath and capped with the Imperial Crown was put up by Nichols' Bonapartist son-in-law as an elaborate tease based on the proprietor's own initial. Poor Nichols had understood that the proposed decoration would commemorate his own name, not that of the hated Napoleon III, and found it difficult to forgive his son-in-law Georges Pigache.

The Café-Restaurant Royal prospered in Glasshouse Street, and in 1870 Nichols took No. 8 Air Street. He employed Arthur Cates to rebuild it, and to alter Nos. 15 and 17 Glasshouse Street and No. 68 Regent Street. There was a billiard room and wine cellar in the basement, a luncheon bar in the front, and a café at the back, on the ground floor, with the kitchen of the restaurant proper on the first floor. On the two floors above were small rooms, possibly originally intended for living accommodation for the staff, but ultimately put to other use. The Café Royal's historian has claimed that Nichols introduced the *salon privé* to London—this is perhaps to overestimate the naïveté of Londoners—and certainly other restaurants provided them in the 1860s. The provision of a discreet private room at short notice was part of the Café Royal service, until it was abruptly ended in 1909. The legend is that a younger member of the Pigache family was so shocked by what went on that he demanded the closing of the upstairs rooms.

In the 1880s and early 1890s the original French artistic patrons of the Café Royal, who included Gustave Doré, were joined by London's leading artists and writers. The Domino Room became the haunt first of Whistler, then of Oscar Wilde and his coterie, a story which has been far too well told elsewhere for repetition here. The reputation of the Café Royal inevitably reflected that of Wilde. Customers were at first attracted by the brilliant journalistic gatherings which included Aubrey Beardsley, William Rothenstein, Ernest Dowson, Max Beerbohm, and Frank Harris the editor of the *Saturday Review*—then repelled by Wilde's disastrous trial and the resulting scandal. The eclipse was only temporary—in the early years of this century the company was again as glittering as before, and the Café's reputation as a gathering place for intellectuals and artists was just as high.

Forty years later, Max Beerbohm remembered going out into Regent Street—'. . . when its wide road and pavements were empty in the dawn, and its level copings were pale against the smokeless sky, the great long curve of the smooth-faced houses had a beauty that I shall not forget . . .' Those were the days before D.O.R.A. (the Defence of the Realm Act, which limited opening hours) or the Catering and Wages Act.

There were a number of wine merchants in the street. J. Carbonnell, for instance, built his own premises, and his firm remained at No. 182 until the end of the nineteenth century. One wine merchant that is still in its original premises at

No. 155 is Hedges and Butler, arguably the descendants of the grocer described by Sala. James Butler, teaman and grocer, moved to Regent Street in 1840, possibly from No. 3 Haymarket, where he had a business as tea dealer and Italian warehouseman. In 1844 he went into partnership with a successful wine merchant William Hedges, whose daughter he married. The Hedges' business as wine merchants had been established in 1667, in the area of the Strand. The later partnership became first an 'Italian warehouse', and finally a wine and spirits merchant only. William Hedges was already a Royal Warrant holder, and the business continued to supply the Royal Family. They supplied champagne to Queen Victoria, and champagne by the 125 dozen, dry gin and orange bitters to the Prince of Wales. They sent champagne and port out to Delhi for the durbar, and Scotch whisky by the hogshead at 23 shillings a gallon in 1911 when King George V returned. They supplied vermouth and rum for the Prince of Wales in 1921. Times changed—300 dozen of champagne were ordered for laying down for the old Queen's cellar in 1886 but by 1932 orders for 3 dozen bottles of rum would be telephoned. The firm supplemented its delivery drays with a lorry in 1905. They carried out cautious experiments such as sending a delivery to Brighton by road and in 1912 they abandoned their horses for motor transport. (See page 94.)

Everything in Regent Street reflected fashion—even the sale of tobacco. In 1842 there were seven tobacconists, by 1870, nine, but their monopoly had been challenged by three cigar importers. By 1890 there were only three tobacconists and twice as many cigar shops. By 1910 there were as few as three shops selling tobacco in any form. The popularity of the cigar shops reflected the service they provided—supplying not only cigars but sherry and a place to smoke. Mrs Carlin's, at No. 189, was the leading establishment of this sort in Regent Street, where in the 1860s various noblemen 'might be seen seated on tobacco tubs and cigar chests, smoking big cigars and drinking sherry which flowed from casks round the shop'.

**Right** Nos. 62–72 the Quadrant, in 1910, with the main entrance of the Café Royal, No. 68 Regent Street.

**Top left** William Hedges (1787–1872).
**Top right** James Butler (1811–1882).
**Centre** New Burlington Mews, 1905. A number of firms had mews accommodation for horses and transport, or for workshops, until the rebuilding. Hedges and Butler also had extensive cellarage behind and under their shop in Regent Street.
**Below** Hedges and Butler Ltd., 153–155 Regent Street, 1905, showing the firm's first motor transport.
**Far right** The Hanover Chapel about 1890.

It was, however, fashion in clothing, and to a large extent women's fashion, that made Regent Street important, that attracted the long lines of carriages at the kerb, that brought the concert programmes into the music shops and the sellers of bouquets and lapdogs to stand on the pavements.

The fashion shops first sold materials, buttons and trimmings for home dressmaking, and only much later in the century, ready-made clothes. Dressmakers and the rather grander court dressmakers increased enormously in the 1890s to about 17, from only a handful in the 1840s and 1870s. There were only eight in 1910, but this reflected the increase of dress departments in the big stores. By this time Swan and Edgar had abandoned their original style of silk mercers and dealers in fine materials, and had become 'costumiers'. Tailors were of course working largely for men, though women's riding habits were also made by tailors, and an increasing number of ladies' tailors made their appearance. In addition to the silk mercers, woollen drapers, linen drapers, lacemen and button sellers, who provided the materials, there were a number of specialist shops which supplied fans, gloves, hats, umbrellas, underwear and, of course, corsets. The number of corset makers remained steady at six or eight, but was supplemented by those ladies' outfitters who also sold underwear, and by the larger stores who were selling corsets by the 1890s.

For fans, if one could afford it, one went to Duvelleroy, at No. 167, established in the late 1850s as the Paris branch of an artistic fan maker, supplying hand-painted fans by well known artists like Gavarni and Eugène Lami, or Messrs Piver, who combined fan making with perfumery. For umbrellas there was Sangster, again a branch establishment but a branch of an English business founded in 1777 in Fleet Street and which flourished at No. 140 from 1839 until the 1920s. There were a number of brush and comb makers in the early days and their trade was often combined with perfumery. This also went with a glover's trade, and later on, in the 1890s, with hairdressing. The growth of the hairdressing business, like that of dressmaking, reflects the growth in the number of prosperous middle class women who no longer had a ladies' maid who could perform all these useful tasks. Perfumery could also be combined with the business of a chemist, like that of Morny Frères, at No. 201, in 1910. Savory and Moore, already established in Bond Street, must have been the first chemist in Regent Street. They were paying rates at No. 220 in 1826 as Savory Moore and Davidson, a name that changed to John Savory, then to Savory and Moore, until they vanished from the street in the 1850s.

The larger shop of the nineteenth century was known as a warehouse, and there were specialist warehouses up and down Regent Street in the 1840s. There were warehouses for mantles and shawls, while others reflected the origin of the goods rather than their character, being Irish (linen and lace), Oriental or Scotch.

**Top** Liberty's premises at Chesham House, Nos. 142–6, sold carpets, curtains and furnishings; at Nos. 148–154 one could buy 'artistic furniture and bric-a-brac'.
**Above** Arthur Lazenby Liberty, (1843–1917). ' . . . he has brought this beauty within the reach of the poor as well as the rich, and what William Morris did for us in the way of wallpapers etc., he has done for us in the matter of carpets, curtain hangings, and dress fabrics . . .'
**Right** Liberty and Co.: furnishings, and 'artistic furniture' from catalogues.

The most famous of the Scotch or Tartan warehouses in Regent Street was Scott Adie, who established themselves in 1854 on the prominent corner site at No. 115. By 1860 they displayed the Royal Warrant, and proclaimed grandly that they were linsey-woolsey manufacturers to Her Majesty. Their range had grown immensely from the shepherd's plaids which had started the Scotch craze in the 1830s. They offered tweeds in Highland, heather and granite mixtures, Shetland shawls, Scotch hosiery, Perth lawns and linens. They also sold such exotics as tartan spun and glacé silks, and silky vicuna fabrics whose only connection with Scotland seems to have been that the wool was prepared by prisoners in Elgin gaol.

Oriental warehouses overlapped somewhat with shops selling shawls, since many of the finest of the these came from India. Shawls were very popular in the early Victorian era, since it was difficult to wear a mantle over the more elaborate crinolines. Sala remembered J. & J. Holmes at Nos. 171–175, who sold nothing but cashmere shawls of the most expensive kinds, some costing as much as 150 guineas. Their large establishment was taken over by Farmer and Rogers, who took on a young man in 1862 called Arthur Lazenby Liberty, who was to become the best known oriental warehouseman of all time.

Arthur Liberty started work at 18, and was so successful that at 21 he was managing the shop. It was the beginning of the enthusiasm for all things Japanese which was taken up by interior decorators and artists, and which was lampooned in the pages of *Punch* and on the stage in the comic opera *The Mikado*. The oriental warehouse attracted famous artists and leaders of artistic fashion like Whistler, Rossetti, and Burne-Jones, and when Farmer and Rogers closed in 1875, these men encouraged the young manager to set up on his own, opposite at No. 218a.

His business prospered and also grew enormously in scope. As he explained many years later, he was almost forced to take on other departments. His oriental furniture and china needed artistic furniture to partner it in English homes, so the firm gradually developed its own extensive workshops. Genuine oriental fabrics and shawls were very costly so he turned to the British textile industry for home-produced textiles with the same lightness and elegance and aesthetic appeal. He commissioned designs by important artists, creating a 'house style' so distinct and internationally famous that it was said that the French never spoke of '*soie* Liberty, the latter word alone is all sufficing'.

Success brought its own problems—the new light materials with their fashionable aesthetic colours were disliked by the British dressmaker: '. . . She was accustomed to work on hard stiff lines, and the new material gave her more trouble . . .' Liberty turned to an architect and stage designer E. W. Godwin to provide dress designs, and was forced to open his own dressmaking and fashion departments, which were scattered up and down Regent Street.

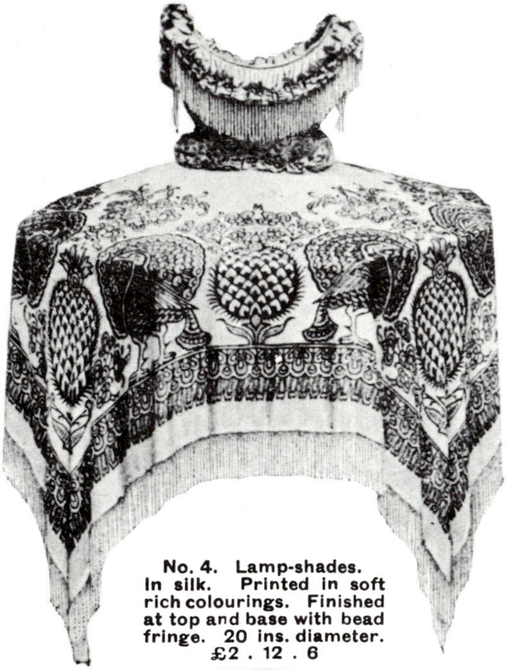

**No. 4. Lamp-shades. In silk. Printed in soft rich colourings. Finished at top and base with bead fringe. 20 ins. diameter. £2 . 12 . 6**

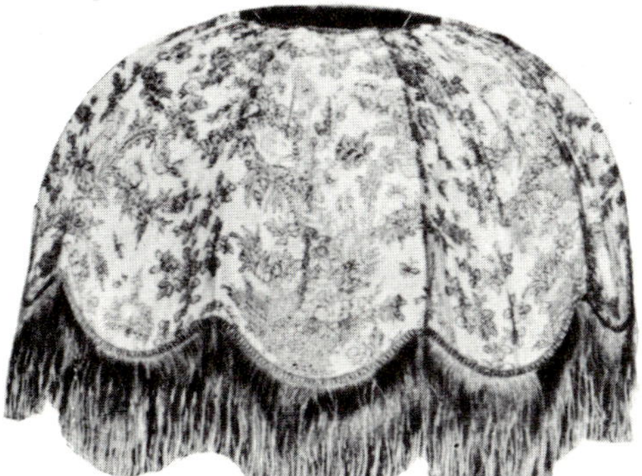

**Kilted Tulle Ruffle,** *as illustration,* with Ribbon Petals and long ends of Oriental Satin Ribbon.
Made in all Black, and also in White with Black Ribbon. **Price 21/9**

Any color to order. **Price 39/6**

**Box pleated Tulle Ruffles** in Black or White. **Price from 15/9**

In colors from **21/9**

**Left** Jay's in 1910 at Nos. 243–253, on the south-east side of Oxford Circus. Despite an attempt to branch out into 'artistic creations', its reputation was still largely funereal:
*'Now the aunt you dearly cherished*
*Through her long declining days*
*Leaves a legacy that will not*
*Pay the mourning bills at Jays.'*
H.T. Lyon in *Owed to Spring*

**Below** Advertisement for Peter Robinson, Mourning Warehouse, 1901.
**Right** Dickins and Jones's premises at Nos. 224–244 Regent Street in 1913. They moved from the sign of the Golden Lion at No. 54 Oxford Street in 1835, bringing their golden lion with them. In the intervening years it seems to have had a sizeable litter. The rounded end to the block was designed, presumably by Nash himself, to balance the rounded end of the Harmonic Institution on the opposite corner. He was presumably responsible for the rather heavy, self-consciously architectural design of the rest of the group.

Artistic courage and enthusiasm brought Arthur Liberty both renown and commercial success to an unusual degree. In Norman Shaw's words to him: 'You have put your mark on your time—like Pugin, Whistler, and fortunately some others. You found things—most of them beastly, and you leave them glorious in colour and full of interest!'

Liberty and Company provided the wherewithal for one of the most important revolutions in British living at the end of the nineteenth century, a revolution which had a much wider impact than any fashion sold elsewhere in the street. This was an interesting foretaste of the way in which fashions in clothes, textiles, and furniture would become important to the growing professional class, to the middle class wives of Kensington and Hampstead and to the suburban homes in Birmingham and Manchester. This was clearly reflecting a transfer of money and influence from the aristocracy to the middle class. Arthur Liberty's death was an event of national impact, and provincial papers like the *Birmingham Mail* noticed: 'To him we owe in a large measure the dethronement of the 'set' rooms, with their ugly and stiff furniture and hangings, and in their place he gave us the present-day comfortable chairs and healthful textiles and ornaments which have transformed the home . . .'

If fashion was important to the Victorians, the ritualistic observance of death had almost greater appeal. Regent Street had two important mourning warehouses, Messrs Jays at No. 247 and the mourning branch of Peter Robinson at Nos. 256–262. There was even a widow's milliner at No. 294. The mourning warehouse was one of the earliest forms of ready-to-wear shops—Nicholson's, who opened the Argyll General Mourning and Mantle Warehouse in the 1850s offered 'every requisite for a complete outfit of mourning . . . at a moment's notice . . .'.

The most important mourning warehouse was that of W. C. Jay, synonymous with mourning for the Edwardians, though they branched out into 'artistic creations' of a non-funereal sort as the century progressed. Established on a prominent site at No. 247 Regent Street in 1841, they gradually extended into the Circus itself, taking over their final site of six houses, Nos. 243–53, by 1880. Here they had mantles, caps, bonnets and streamers, silks, muslins, velvets and silks and satins for every grade of mourning, from deepest black to pale lavender, worn by those emerging from the period of strict mourning. Workshops, both for bespoke and ready-made clothing, were also on the premises. Henry Mayhew, who paid a visit there in 1865, observed that 'in the present day . . . our grief goes for nothing if not fashionable'.

Peter Robinson started as a linen draper at 103 Oxford Street in 1833, and gradually expanded not only into mourning but also into men's outfitting, into boys' clothing at No. 278, and the manufacture of portmanteaux at No. 286 on the corner of Great Castle Street by 1890. At its greatest extent the store dominated the northern circus, with men's and boys' outfitting on the north-eastern side and women's fashions and mourning on the south side, where Peter Robinson had taken over the old-established linen drapers and silk mercers, Hodge and Lowman, at Nos. 256–262.

In contrast, Dickins and Jones's premises were always more concentrated, slowly spreading out to include all the shops between Argyll Place and Little Argyll Street. Though they stuck to their title of silk mercers till 1910, they already supplied every aspect of ladies' fashions in the 1890s.

Swan and Edgar is the oldest drapery business in Regent Street, and from their original premises at Nos. 9 and 10 they expanded rapidly both into the Circus and the Quadrant. By 1848 they occupied Nos. 45–51 in the Quadrant, and all that corner of Piccadilly Circus, except for a group of travel and

MUNYON
270
HOVIS
PETER ROBINSON
PETER ROBINSON
PETER ROBINSON

**Left** Regent Circus and Oxford Street in the 1890s, the last decade of horse-drawn London. The need for more space forced many shops to expand upwards; it was usually done tactfully, as here, by Peter Robinson Ltd.
**Below** Swan and Edgar in 1910.

telegraph offices. In 1841 they built a splendid new shopfront, much admired by contemporaries for its architectural character, and which provided room for display behind its great-plate glass windows. Even amongst drapers' shops renowned for their important fascias, brilliant lighting and showy dressing, the new Swan and Edgar's premises stood out. Dressing the shop windows was done every day in high class shops, and because of this, and long working hours of about 60 hours a week, employees had to live near their work. In small establishments the apprentices and junior staff lived with the family, and at larger establishments they lived in dormitories above the shops. This accommodation was a standard part of large Victorian stores, and even at Swan and Edgar's, where the pressure on space was particularly great, it was only ended in 1900. The annual office party also seems to have been a more paternalistic affair in those days, for Sala recalled hearing Mr Edgar's employees cheering him at the annual dinner.

William Edgar (1791–1869) was the son of a Cumberland farmer. He had come to London about 1814, where he had worked for George Swan, a Ludgate draper, at his new Piccadilly branch, and been taken into partnership, becoming sole proprietor on George Swan's death in 1821. He became extremely successful—he bought himself a large suburban house in Clapham, and produced a large family, most of whom married well. Only W. S. Edgar (1824–1883) went into the business, again a successful but not revolutionary figure. His son Lewis earned more renown for his horsemanship than for his capacities as a shopkeeper: 'That damned draper', growled a fellow clubman, 'is the finest whip in London.'

The firm passed out of the family hands, amalgamating with a firm called Waterloo House in 1886, and became a limited company with the unwieldy title of Waterloo House and Swan and Edgar Ltd. By 1900 they dominated Piccadilly Circus, proudly calling the north-west quadrant 'Swan and Edgar's Corner'. Their important situation as leaseholders was to make them important

**Left** The Rusitor, by Burberry, 1913, designed for the traveller or motorist, and claimed to 'combine the cosiness of a dressing-gown with all the external attributes demanded by the highest standards of good taste'.
**Top right** Hamleys, the famous toy shop at No. 200 Regent Street in 1910. The firm was first established at No. 64 in the 1890s.
**Bottom right** The Goldsmiths' and Silversmiths' Company showroom about 1890.

protagonists in the coming battle over the redevelopment of the Circus and the Quadrant.

H. J. and D. Nicoll at Nos. 114–118 succeeded the 'great drapery establishment' of William Hitchcock in the 1840s. They started business as army clothiers, and then became tailors to both men and women, making their name as inventors of the paletot. By the 1880s, according to Alison Adburgham's authoritative history *Shops and Shopping*, they ranked among the dozen leading fashionable dressmakers, almost *couturiers* in modern terms, though they preferred the title of merchant tailors. They were among the first stores to rebuild in Regent Street, remaining at the same address till after the Second World War, when they were taken over by Montague Burton.

Men's tailors also made riding habits, and often rainproof and waterproof coats for women as well. Two names which have passed into the English language are Aquascutum and Burberry. Regent Street always seems to have had one or two macintosh or waterproof clothing manufacturers—as necessary as umbrellas in the English climate. Burberry's were established in the Haymarket by 1901. Samuel Bax, macintosh manufacturer of No. 48 Regent Street, patented a showerproof woollen fabric some time in the 1840s and this was shown at the Great Exhibition. Soon after, the shop was sold, together with the patent rights to the 'aquascutum wrapper', to John Emary. Englishmen, from officers going to the Crimea to the Prince of Wales himself, adopted Emary's clothes. The shop was swept away for the making of Piccadilly Circus but the business moved to 100 Regent Street. It went through a series of ownerships until it was decided to adopt the name of its most famous product—Aquascutum.

Tailors were always important in Regent Street, numbering about 15 in 1842, then about 20 in 1870 and 1890, and rising to about 24 in 1910, about eleven of whom were ladies' tailors such as Phillips, Solomon Fisher, and Hart and Co.

Men's fashions were also represented by leading hatters like Melton, Johnson and Perring, and most of the bootmakers worked for men. Boots and shoes were mainly bespoke at this period and the first shoe companies to sell ready-to-wear shoes emerged in the last decade of the nineteenth century. The American Shoe Company on the corner of New Burlington Street demonstrated the more aggressive nature of the retailing to come, by contrast with the more retiring attitude of such older firms as N. Thierry, who were bootmakers established at No. 70 in 1839.

**Far left** Aquascutum: as advertised in *Country Life,* 1913.
**Bottom left** Mr Perring's mobile advertisement described in 1843 as 'a colossal hat mounted upon springs like a gig . . . which may still be remembered – perhaps still seen – dashing down Regent Street at the heels of a spirited horse . . .'
**Left** Mr Emary, (1810–1897), of 46 and 48 Regent Street, owner of the 'Aquascutum' patent.
**Below** The corner of New Burlington Street and the west side of Regent Street in 1912, a small corner invaded by American firms. Between the American Shoe Company and Buttericks, were the showrooms of Eastman Kodak. Buttericks set up their paper pattern business in Regent Street in 1873 at No. 177. By the 1880s they had taken over the whole of Farmer and Rogers shawl warehouse next door at 171–5, and set up a nationwide system of agents.

Furriers and plumassiers provided a small but important contingent in the army of fashion retailers. Fur was first used for linings and for carriage rugs. From a very early time, there were furriers in Regent Street, but the two most prominent Edwardian ones were Swears and Wells, at No. 192, and the International Fur Company with its engaging bear, established in the 1880s at Nos. 163–5. Swears and Wells started at the Lilliputian warehouse at No. 192 some time before 1862, and only expanded at the end of the century, finally occupying Nos. 190–196. There were other fashionable furriers like Revillon Frères and the Imperial Fur Company, but the fur trade was not central to Regent Street.

Drapers and tailors as well as furriers needed workshops above their premises, and many attic storeys were rebuilt to provide enlarged windows for the extra light needed for the close sewing. As the pressure on West End space increased, more work was sent out, particularly from those in the tailoring trade. High class English tailors had the work carried out on the premises but the ready-made tailoring trade always depended more on tailoring done in the workshops in the East End.

Jewellery was another trade closely allied to the rest of the fashion industry. It was always well represented by some dozen or so jewellers in any year throughout the nineteenth century, and by a smaller number of clock and watchmakers. The tendency was broadly the same—a gradual movement from the manual craftsman to the large composite organisation represented at the end of

**Top left** Nos. 122–132 Regent Street, in 1910, including the premises of three famous shops: Carringtons, Negretti and Zambra, and Jaeger.
**Bottom left** Jaeger and Co. Ltd., Corsets: Ariel.
**Top right** Dr Gustav Jaeger, inventor of the Sanitary Woollen System of clothing. His woollen clothes were very popular with explorers, being taken by Nansen to the Arctic, and Scott to the Antarctic, and also by Stanley on his expedition to Equatorial Africa, in 1887.
**Bottom right** James Lillywhite (1825–1882), founder of the Lillywhite's sports shop, from a print published by his brother.

Trade Mark.

the century by such distinguished firms as the Goldsmiths and Silversmiths Company, Carrington and Company, J. C. Vickery, and Mappin and Webb.

Packer and Company, at No. 78, represented a smaller type of firm. They had started at No. 78 the Quadrant some time before 1842, and had expanded into No. 76 by 1862 where they remained throughout the century.

Elkington, the pioneers in electroplate, were established early in Lower Regent Street. They took over J. G. Fearn's goldsmiths' shop at No. 22 in the 1840s and remained there until the 1920s.

Hardly decorative but certainly all the rage was Dr Jaeger's Sanitary Woollen System, based on his theory propounded in a series of lectures in the 1870s, of the superiority of wool over vegetable mixtures as human clothing. The system was promoted by the English agent, L. R. S. Tomalin, who opened the first shop in Princes Street in 1883. The system was very popular with the public, being adopted by progressive intellectuals like Bernard Shaw. A branch was opened in Regent Street in the 1890s, where sanitary woollen clothing could be obtained for man and beast, in all shapes and forms from corsets to horse blankets.

Jaeger's success was due to the increasing interest in both health and sport. One of the first retail shops devoted to catering for the new interest in outdoor sports of all kinds was opened by James Lillywhite in 1863. Lillywhite was one of three brothers, all well known in the cricketing world, sons of Frederick William Lillywhite (1792–1854), a famous Sussex cricketer. All three brothers were involved with the cricketing world—John had a bat-making business, and Fred a portable printing press with which he attended matches and even foreign cricketing tours! As the range of sports open to the leisured English middle class grew, so did Lillywhite's business—cricket, croquet, football, golf, tennis, all contributed so that by 1925, the shop at 31 Haymarket was outgrown, and the firm took part of the Criterion building on the corner of Piccadilly Circus and Lower Regent Street.

## Traffic in Regent Street

'Regent Street is full of handsome shops, and during the afternoon, in the height of the London season is the very centre of fashion, and with its show of fine carriages, horses and gay company, forms one of the most striking sights of the metropolis.'

The sketch from the *Illustrated London News* shows how great was the congestion caused by wealthy shoppers arriving in their carriages. It is not really surprising since Regent Street was not only 'a happy hunting ground for ardent shoppers' but also a major north-south traffic route. In addition, the Life Guards, whose barracks were in Regent's Park in the early part of the century, rode down Regent Street to Whitehall and St James's every morning at eleven o'clock. On the Queen's Drawing room days the band played during the reception and therefore wore ceremonial uniform.

Occasionally there were other processions, as when the trade union operatives marched down Regent Street in 1832, or when the wedding procession of the Duke and Duchess of Edinburgh passed down it in 1874. On the whole, however, the congestion in Regent Street seems to have been a commonplace of West End life:
'All is dizzying confusion,' the *Illustrated London News* told its readers in 1866, 'the fireflies of fashion glance rapidly hither and thither, and the West-end street is thronged with a jumble of carriages, horsemen and horsewomen, cabs, omnibuses and waggons; the pavements being crowded with fashionable loungers'.

The very grandest way to do one's shopping in Regent Street was in a carriage and pair, complete with coachman and the omnipresent footman, but this sort of extravagance was not for everyone. The range of expense for the private carriage owner was very wide; in 1893, it was estimated that a chariot could cost 300 guineas, though a pony trap would be a mere fifteen, while a pair of horses fit for a state coach could cost eight hundred guineas, as against a twenty-guinea pony. When preferred one could 'job' one's horses, that is hire them from one of the many jobmasters who ran large stables, contracting to supply horses and carriages to 'carriage folk' at so much a year, or sometimes at so much a week just for the season. In this case, one could hire brougham and horse for £200 a year. Private carriages paid tax, and it was estimated in 1891 that there were some 22,000 private carriages licensed in London.

It seems unlikely that women often went shopping in Regent Street on horseback, but there were a surprising number of riders in London in 1866. The number of ridden horses lessened in London throughout Queen Victoria's reign as public transport became better organised and cheaper. It has been estimated that equestrians equalled carriages in number at the beginning of the reign, but decreased in number after the beginning of the 1880s.

The two standbys of the Victorian cab trade were the hansom 'patent safety' cab invented in 1834, and the four-wheeler, of which an improved version came on the market the following year. The hansom had two very large wheels and was said to be safer and less hard on the horse than the four-wheeler. The latter was for a family party with luggage, while the hansom carried two only and was driven by the cabman from behind the passengers. A well-kept hansom was described as an elegant sight: 'swaying delicately in unison with the horse, the whip poised like a lance in its holder, and to protect the enamel on the top of the cab, the cotton summer cover in colours or white with tassels, made in most cases by the cabby's wife, as the wives of the gondolieri still make covers for the cabin-tops.'

In 1896, there were 7,585 hansoms licensed in London and only 3,449 four-wheelers. Both kinds of cabs made themselves a nuisance by 'crawling' in search of fares down busy streets, so this was forbidden in important thoroughfares, and they had to wait on ranks like those in Upper Regent Street. These ranks were fairly strictly regulated—an Act of 1843 made it obligatory to have a man in attendance to water the horses; it was not until 1875 that the first cabman's shelter serving a hot meal for the cabbies appeared! By 1900 there were about 45 cab shelters including one near the Langham Hotel, of which a number were provided by various charities.

Cabs were owned by companies as well as by individuals, though the Metropolitan Police licence without which the cabby was not allowed to ply for hire was issued to the individual not to the

**Left** Portrait of the Prince Regent, from a study in oils by Sir Thomas Lawrence. *Plate XIII*

**Below** The Quadrant, Regent Street, in 1822, from a drawing by T. H. Shepherd, for Ackermann's series of aquatints. *Plate XIV*

The Quadrant, Regent Street in 1852, after the removal of the colonnades and balconies in 1848. Swan and Edgar's new window is on the lefthand side. *Plate XV*

COUNTY FIRE OFFICE
REGENT STREET
HINDOSTAN

**Above** Cumberland Terrace in 1840. *Plate XVI*

**Right** Interior of the Colosseum, 1836. *Plate XVII*

These two engravings were fashion plates published by B. Read of Hart Street, Bloomsbury Square, and Broad Way, New York, America. He used the Park and its buildings as the background for a number of years.

**Left** Upper Regent Street with a row of cabs waiting, about 1900. There was a cabman's shelter at the top of the street near the Langham Hotel.

company. An alternative system was for the individual cabby to hire his cab and horse from the company at a rate which varied with the season, often rebated in the event of bad weather and bad luck. In the 1890s the rate of nine shillings a day in the winter months rose to a shilling a day from April to the end of May, reaching the annual peak of eighteen shillings a day for the brief height of the season, which lasted during Derby week till the end of the second week in June. The rate then dropped by a shilling a week till it reached nine shillings, the standard winter rate. The curve of the hire charge for cab and horse reveals, like nothing else, the briefness of the period during which the fashionable Victorian reckoned to be in London with his family.

The cab companies pioneered a number of improvements, such as india-rubber tyres, introduced by the aristocratic Shrewsbury-Talbot Cab Company.

Cheaper public transport was provided by the horse bus. The first omnibus had been introduced by a young stable keeper called Shillibeer in 1829, when he pioneered a service between Paddington and the Bank. This sort of conveyance was drawn by three horses and carried no passengers outside. In due course, as the roads became better maintained the number of passengers increased and the buses were drawn by only two horses. In the 1840s the new 'knifeboard' buses were introduced with twelve passengers inside and ten on top, to be superseded by the garden seat type.

The stage coaches ran along Piccadilly where there were a number of coaching inns—the White Bear, the White Horse Cellar, the Gloucester Coffee House, and Hatchetts and Webb's Hotels, and the Bull and Mouth western office, the Piccadilly office of one of the large City coachmasters. With the opening of the railways, the coaching traffic fell off, though there was a somewhat sentimental revival in the 1870s when aristocratic and well-to-do owners horsed and drove short distance coaches to places like Brighton (see Plate XVII).

The omnibus routes naturally took in important destinations like railway stations, but the railway companies often ran buses from their central booking offices or the old coaching inns to the termini, often by arrangement with the omnibus companies.

The Metropolitan Railway was opened from Paddington to Farringdon Road in 1863, and shortly afterwards the Company began a 'feeder' service from Regent Circus to their Portland Road station, now Great Portland Street. They had an office in Regent Circus, Oxford Street, and extended the service to Piccadilly in 1874.

The railway buses were much larger than the others, being divided into first and second class accommodation, and being drawn by three horses. They were very distinctive, and also carried an umbrella with 'Metropolitan Railway' on it.

The route was extended from Piccadilly Circus on to Charing Cross in 1883, and then gradually curtailed, until the service between Piccadilly Circus and Baker Street was ended in 1894. The big buses then ran between Piccadilly Circus and the new Metropolitan terminus at Baker Street, until 1900, when the service was withdrawn.

With all these horses, the streets were naturally

filthy, and a busy trade was plied, particularly on wet days, by crossing sweepers. These might be invalid soldiers, women or children who were given a tip for sweeping the major street crossings by passers-by. In well-organised residential areas a square might have its 'own' crossing sweeper who would be employed by the servants in the big houses to run errands and so forth, and who probably received a small regular sum from the householders. In important thoroughfares like Regent Street, however, a pitch was a valuable possession and jealously guarded. A twelve-year-old girl, whom Henry Mayhew met, described how she had decided to take up crossing sweeping, encouraged by the number of sweepers earning a living in this way in Regent Street. Trafalgar Square was swept by a gang of boys and girls, who shared the sweeping and had a sort of childish system of 'bagging' the tips from passers-by. There do not seem to have been any such syndicates in Regent Street—possibly the crossings were so remunerative that adults took charge of the sweeping there.

In 1899 came an innovation which was to revolutionise the London scene—the first petrol bus took to the road in London. Within twelve years the internal combustion engine had replaced horse-drawn buses and the taxi was rapidly taking over from the hansom cab. It was an incredibly swift revolution throughout the world of transport, though private carriages and tradesman's vehicles survived longer than any form of public transport. State coaches, the very grand coaches used only for royal and diplomatic receptions, virtually disappeared between the coronations of Edward VII and George V. In 1902 during a long reception at the India Office there was a line down Whitehall of the empty carriages standing at right angles to the kerb, with the horses taken out. In 1911 there were hardly half a dozen left to join the Coronation procession.

The Central London Railway, known as 'the Tuppenny Tube', was opened in 1900, with a short system running from the Royal Exchange to Shepherd's Bush. It had a station at Oxford Circus, on the east side of Argyll Street, of no great architectural distinction, finished in the terracotta fashionable for underground stations at the time.

In 1906 the Waterloo and Baker Street Railway opened a station on the other side of Argyll Street, designed by the architect to the railway, Leslie W. Green, again using glazed terracotta as a facing material.

These two underground railways proved a valuable new source of transport. Surface traffic had been remarkably heavy since the 1890s when it was said of the area, 'known as Oxford Circus or Regent Circus indifferently. Some of the best shops in London are to be found here; the traffic from early morning until night is enormous, and would prove a source of danger to pedestrians were it not for the admirable system of police supervision . . .'

**Left** Looking down Lower Regent Street to Waterloo Place in the 1890s. On the left hand side of the road are Nash's own house, the pedimented group of Carlton Chambers, and the Junior United Service Club on the corner of Charles Street.
**Below** Regent Circus North and the top of Regent Street about 1900.

JASCHKE
COUNTY FIRE OFFICE
St. MARY'S WHARF PADD 6020
EXCAVATIONS SAND, BALLAST

# IV The rebuilding of Regent Street: 1904-1928

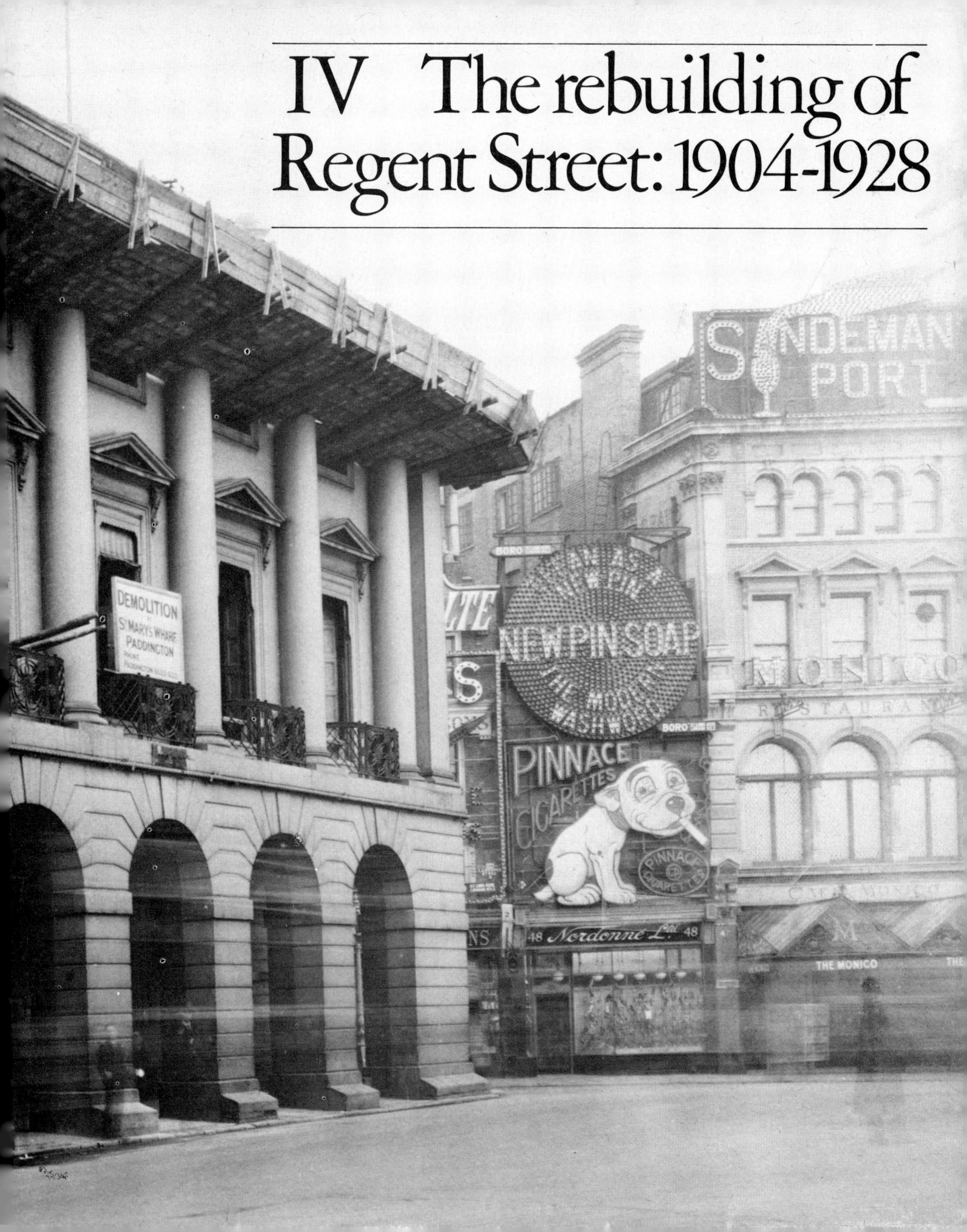

## Norman Shawism run mad . . . '

By the reign of Edward VII, Regent Street had enjoyed eighty years of trading as the 'centre of fashion', as a street so dependent on society for its custom that out of season it 'assimilated to Pompeii in its loneliness'. By 1907, however, change was in the wind, and with change came problems for the shopkeepers.

The first of these problems was the centennial redevelopment, something that was understood and anticipated by every prudent London leaseholder, who put by money for rebuilding well in advance. Nonetheless, redevelopment presented a threat, particularly to the small trader: 'all the small men will be turned out into the street, as shops are not like removing in private houses, and the loss of business at any removal is bad enough even a few doors away'.

The second problem was a change in the nature of the customers in Regent Street, partly due to a shift in the relative wealth of the aristocracy and the middle classes. This trend had been encouraged by heavier taxation and was reflected in such portents as the sale of important pictures to American buyers, and even the dismantling of country houses for the same purpose. The demolition of West End palaces had begun—the Duke of Portland's house in Cavendish Square, Harcourt House, had been pulled down in 1906 after being empty for 20 years, the Earl of Harewood had sold his Adam house in Hanover Square to the Royal Agricultural Society of England for offices in 1895. Early discussions for the redevelopment of Regent Street had proposed blocks of flats on the French model above the shops, but these were dismissed, partly for technical reasons to do with daylighting angles, and partly, one suspects, because it was generally acknowledged that the West End was becoming increasingly non-residential.

These trends meant that the Regent Street shops had to cater for a different kind of customer: in the words of a prominent, but anonymous, shopkeeper to the *Daily Telegraph*:

'. . . from the suburbs and country visitors. A most valuable class of customer, as I said, but in the main they are ladies who want things in quite the most up-to-date style at a very moderate outlay. That means just two important factors to the shopkeeper. In the first place, he must use a cheaper kind of material, on which there is only a small margin of profit, and secondly he is unable to recoup himself on the cost of making up . . . one has to do at least five times the volume of business to get the same returns, and even then the net profits are less.'

It is against this background of diminishing margins that the fierce opposition to the Crown's initial attempt at a uniform rebuilding scheme for Regent Street and the Quadrant must be seen.

It was already clear, not only to those involved in the street but to outsiders that rebuilding was necessary. Professor Kerr told the R.I.B.A. in 1894: '. . . the times had changed while the businesses had not; business had advanced, and the accommodation was left wofully [*sic*] behind. The little shops, once so ample, had had to take in not only the back parlours, but every inch of the back gardens; what had been kitchen-offices were now warehouse basements; and as for the residential accommodation above, not only had it been abandoned in that capacity, but a new tenant would give as much for the shop alone as for the entire house, so that the upper stories, with their miserable staircases, were either utilised for workrooms and storage, or let off contemptuously for what they would fetch. The shops when enlarged to the utmost, were grouped together in twos and threes, adjoining houses in back streets were absorbed, and the cry was for more space. All this time the structural stability of the houses, never good, had been so tried by alterations, that public attention was now and then called to the appearance of danger; and as for sanitary questions, the less said the better. The failure of a street was a familiar phenomenon; but here was prosperity with a vengeance.'

Rebuilding had already been allowed on the sites of the two churches and, of course, many of the tenants were making their own plans. However, the first rebuilding in the Quadrant itself came with the redevelopment of the St James's Hall complex between Regent Street and Piccadilly. This site was taken by a company called the P & R Syndicate who planned to build the Piccadilly Hotel. The hall had been badly hit by the success of the Queen's Hall in Langham Place, while the success of César Ritz's Carlton and Ritz Hotels and

**Right** The west side of Regent Street north of Conduit Street in 1914.

**Previous page** The County Fire Office being demolished in 1924

the rebuilding of the Berkeley Hotel pointed the way to a new series of hotel developments in the Piccadilly area. The promoters of the new hotel employed W. Emden and William Woodward to design their hotel, which was to occupy important Piccadilly and Regent Street frontages, though it was understood that in the Quadrant the design would have to accord with a new uniform design to be selected in due course by the Commissioners.

The Treasury were already concerned about the redevelopment of the whole Regent Street area, and were only too well aware of the public outcry that could result from a wrong decision on such a prominent site. To guard against trouble, therefore, they suggested the appointment of an expert committee to advise the Commissioners of Woods. The members were Aston Webb, President of the Royal Institute of British Architects, John Belcher, designer of a number of interesting commercial buildings, and Sir John Taylor, former Chief Architect to the Office of Works. These architects considered a scheme prepared by Arthur Green, the Commissioners' own Architect, before his death in 1904, and came to the conclusion that it needed revision by 'an architect of eminence'. They suggested Richard Norman Shaw (1831–1912), by then retired from active practice and best-known for his 'fantastic Queen Anne houses' in Chelsea and Hampstead, a number of country houses, and of course, his impressive New Scotland Yard blocks for the Metropolitan Police on the Embankment. He produced a distinguished design for the two façades of the Piccadilly Hotel, which was quite well received by the *cognoscenti*, and also a new layout and complete new scheme for Piccadilly Circus. There is a monumental splendour about his design for the Circus, which he turned from Nash's small-scale elegant, self-contained, pause in a long urban progression into a 'place' on the Parisian model. He managed to ignore most of the practical considerations on such a site, such as the ownership of the land and the existing layout of the streets.

The designs for the Piccadilly Hotel façades were unpopular, most of all with the Syndicate's own architects, who would have to plan the interior behind them, so Shaw revised these, providing his new scheme for the Piccadilly front, with its massive columns, in April 1905. These received the approval of all concerned in six weeks, largely, it has been suggested, because the demolition of the St James's Hall had begun, and the delay would have cost the Syndicate money.

His scheme for the 'circus' has particular interest, in view of its sad recent history. He accepted that the quadrants of the Circus had no further point and that the sensible approach would be to square the end of Swan and Edgar on to the Circus, and also to do away with the curved end to Lower Regent Street. He then made sense of the eastern side of Piccadilly Circus by bringing Shaftesbury Avenue through the Café Monico site and rebuilding the London Pavilion some seventy feet further west to provide a balancing composition for the new Swan and Edgar building.

This scheme was submitted by the Commissioners, somewhat optimistically, to the London County Council for its views on the building lines, and indeed in the hope of active support. This was dashed by Lord Alexander Thynne's letter on behalf of the L.C.C. to George Leveson-Gower, pointing out in May 1909 that 'the cost of interfering with the Pavilion, the Café Monico, or the Piccadilly Mansions is prohibitive . . .' Leveson-Gower wrote back to ask for his help 'in effecting what would really be a splendid public improvement in one of the most important sites in London . . .'

The only result was a call from W. G. Riley, the L.C.C. architect, in the course of which he suggested another scheme, rather more expensive, but with the merit of centralising the unhappily sited Eros in the line of Lower Regent Street.

John Murray (1864–1940) surveyor to the Commissioners of Woods, had been party to a number of these abortive discussions, and finally he produced a scheme of his own, obviously based on Shaw's, but modified in architectural details in the hope of pleasing the shopkeepers. He suggested that this 'circus' should now be called Edward VII Square, in memory of the recently deceased King.

Murray was aware of other proposals for memorials to the King, and he allowed for the presence of both a Shakespeare Memorial Theatre and a National Opera House on the north of the Square. The unhappy Shaftesbury Memorial was to be moved to a new position in a park where it was possible to supply water, and to be replaced by a considerably more substantial statue in bronze and granite, 'the most durable materials for monuments in London'.

Murray's proposal was put to the Lord Mayor,

**Left** The demolition of St James's Hall in 1905.
**Top right** Norman Shaw's scheme for rebuilding both Circus and Quadrant, March 1906.
**Right** W.G. Riley's scheme for reorganising Piccadilly Circus, May 1909.
**Far right** John Murray's plan for King Edward VII Square, 1910.

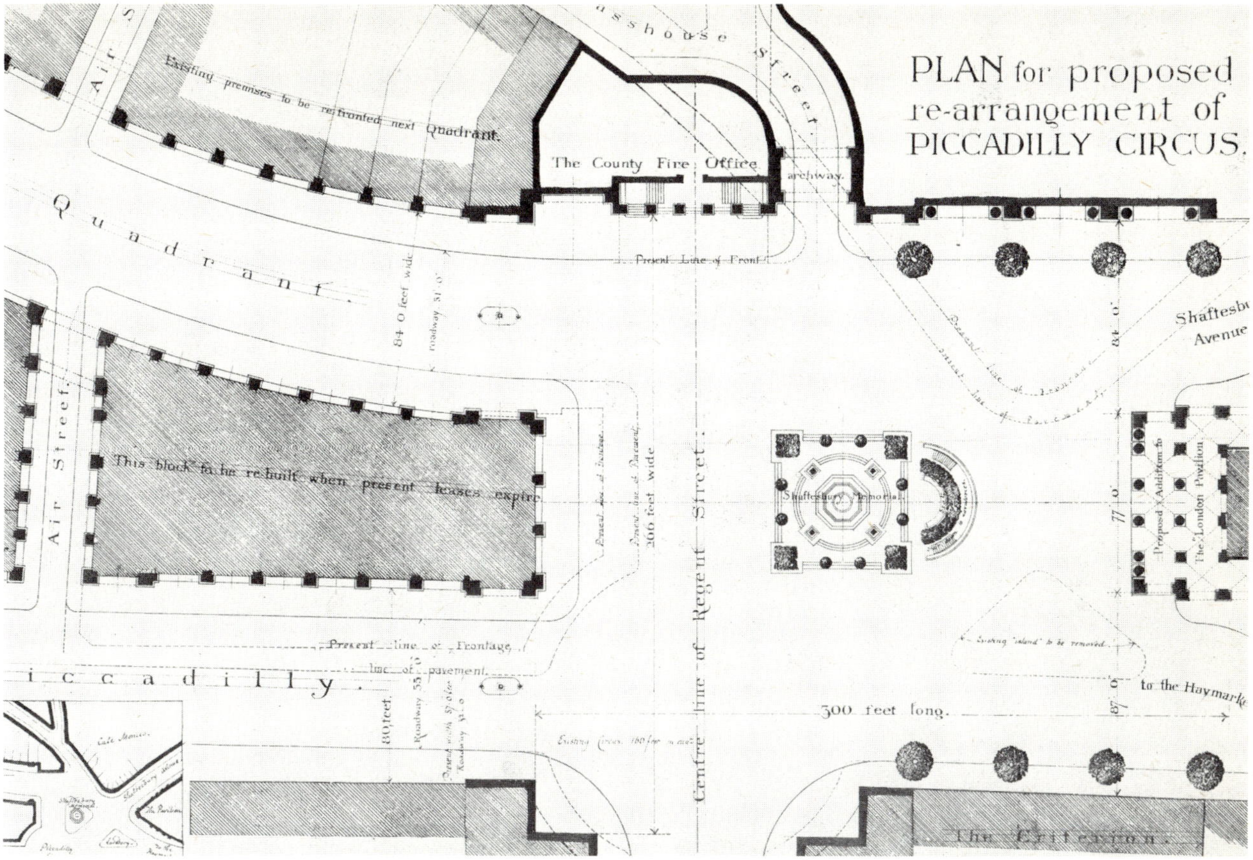
PLAN for proposed
re-arrangement of
PICCADILLY CIRCUS.
Existing premises to be refronted next Quadrant.
The County Fire Office
archway.
Present Line of Front
Quadrant.
84 0 feet wide
Air Street.
This block to be rebuilt when present leases expire.
206 feet wide
Centre line of Regent Street.
Shaftesbury Memorial
Proposed Addition to The London Pavilion
Present line of Frontage
line of pavement.
Piccadilly.
80 feet.
300 feet long.
Existing 'island' to be removed.
The Criterion.
Cafe Monico

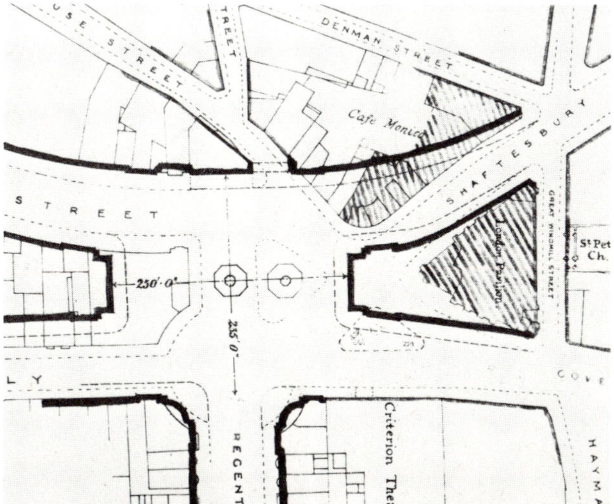
DENMAN STREET
Cafe Monico
SHAFTESBURY
STREET
GREAT WINDMILL STREET
London Pavilion
St Pet Ch.
250' 0"
235' 0"
REGENT STREET
Criterion Theatre
HAYMARKET
JERMYN STREET

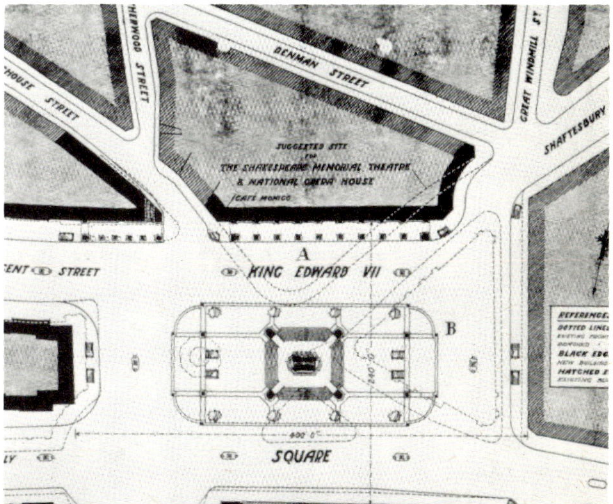
DENMAN STREET
GREAT WINDMILL ST
SHAFTESBURY
SUGGESTED SITE FOR THE SHAKESPEARE MEMORIAL THEATRE & NATIONAL OPERA HOUSE
(CAFE MONICO)
A
KING EDWARD VII
B
400' 0"
SQUARE
CRITERION THEATRE
TUBE RAILWAY STATIONS
HAYMARKET

VIEW OF
KING EDWARD VII SQVARE
LOOKING NORTH-WEST

and his drawings were exhibited with those of Shaw at the Town Planning Conference held in London in 1910. After this, however, his plans, with those of Shaw, were allowed to lapse. Towards the end of his life Blomfield prepared a very similar scheme, exhibited at the Royal Academy in 1936.

In the event, of course, nothing has been done, though the visual squalor has continued to irritate Londoners for more than half a century. The clue to the continuing presence of what Blomfield called 'the disorderly rabble of buildings which at present disgraces the most important "place" in London' lies in the way in which cooperation between local authority and ground landlord has been almost impossible to achieve. Possibly the omens were most favourable in 1909, when the largest landlord in Piccadilly Circus was contemplating redevelopment at a relatively prosperous moment in English history.

We are probably indebted to Shaw for underlining the importance of the County Fire Office site to the Commissioners as the 'finest in London', though they did not respond either to his suggestion that it should be rebuilt on a much deeper site, or to his comment that in Paris they would have made sure that a worthy building went up—even if it cost half a million pounds!

The Piccadilly Hotel was built according to Shaw's designs for the façades, but internally it was planned and designed by Emden and Woodward. The interior decoration was carried out by a number of leading firms which included Goodall of Manchester, responsible for the public rooms, and Liberty's, responsible for the third, fourth and fifth floors. This variety of treatment was deliberate, as the author of *A Twentieth Century Palace* pointed out on the hotel's opening in 1908:

'On the third floor of the hotel and above it (the bedroom suites) almost every known variety of style finds an admirably devised exemplification. The visitor may have a possible preference in this particular direction. If so, he may choose his decorative surroundings, whether his leanings be towards Old English, Adam, Chippendale, Sheraton or Empire, or the more modern school of English design.'

For those with no pronounced leanings the designers thoughtfully provided a bedroom 'the style of which is historically indefinite.'

However, the hotel was less successful financially than artistically, and a receiver was appointed in 1908. The loss was partly due to the difficulty in letting the parade of shops in Regent Street even at a reduced rent. The situation alarmed the other tenants in the Quadrant, who were led by Walter Morford, the articulate and pugnacious managing director of Swan and Edgar's, who had been thoroughly upset by Shaw's design. Indeed, Shaw's designs were a threat to Regent Street shopkeepers outside the Quadrant. His concept was of a uniform style spreading up Regent Street from the Quadrant. As late as October 1908 he was writing to Frederick Hellard at the Office of Woods and Forests:

'. . . and it would be fine if we could have a good frontage . . . with Vigo Street in the centre, and uniform in design—it is 160 feet wide—and that might be a really fine feature . . . we do suffer now-a-days [*sic*] from such terrible raggedness . . . and no comprehensive design to tie the whole thing together . . .'

**Top left** The Piccadilly façade to the Piccadilly Hotel, not carried out quite as originally designed since the gable behind the screen replaced a high mansard roof. This photograph deliberately omits the last two bays, which were not rebuilt to Shaw's design.

**Bottom left** Edward VII Square, as proposed by John Murray in September 1910.

**Left** The County Fire Office. Professor Reilly, writing in 1922, called it 'one of the best short pieces of street architecture we have, strong masculine and unaffected, yet with delightful delicacy in its mesh-like iron balconies.'

The shopkeepers were against the expense of the new design to be carried out in costly Portland stone. They also disliked the height of the new buildings, which they complained made the street dark, and most of all the design of the windows, which made window-dressing difficult and obscured the goods behind the great stone columns. The Commissioners were gravely embarrassed as their brief to Shaw and the prototype building of the Piccadilly Hotel already erected was in direct opposition to the hardening attitude of the shopkeepers. Morford was obdurate—as he told the shareholders of Swan and Edgar in 1909:

'Your directors . . . are absolutely certain that to extend the building which exists . . . on the same elevation would spell ruin to us . . . I would almost . . . say that rather than have such a building . . . we would remove or shut up shop.'

The architect Henry Tanner had been working for tenants on the opposite side of the Quadrant, and he was briefed by Hope Brothers to prepare a design for Nos. 84, 86 and 88, and he then applied it to the whole block between Air Street and Glasshouse Street. Early in 1912 this was submitted to the Commissioners who wrote to the ageing Shaw, in an attempt to enlist his support for Tanner's 'modification'. Shaw was not deceived, and in a dignified letter he resigned all connection with the scheme:

'. . . I was anxious to give the street more or less of a monumental character. As an architect I dwelt much on the piers and arches on pavement level to carry the upper part, but they are gone bodily . . . with all these alterations it can no longer be said to be my design at all.'

Not only were the shopkeepers against Shaw—architectural opinion was also hardening. A correspondent to the *Estates Gazette* wrote in April 1912: 'A beautiful building must be truthful as well as suitable. In addition, the proposed design is not twentieth century architecture: it neither reflects the essential spirit of the age nor modern methods of construction.'

Questions in the House of Commons were followed by a massive newspaper campaign, including fighting words in the *Pall Mall Gazette*, which urged its readers to oppose the 'coterie of officials' who, they alleged, intended 'to ruin the trade and beauty of Regent Street simultaneously—to make a desert and call it Art'. The *Builder* announced a competition for the design of new blocks on either side of the Piccadilly Hotel, which would be approved by the shopkeepers, and would yet accord with Shaw's façade. There was a considerable response to the competition, which was won by the firm of Richardson and Gill in the summer of 1912. They were not, in fact, ever asked to take part in the redevelopment of Regent Street, earning only glory and their modest premium like so many winners of competitions.

The Commissioners bowed to the storm of protest, much of which was couched in unfair and immoderate terms, and later that year appointed yet another committee, headed by Lord Plymouth, a former Commissioner of Works. The members were John Murray, Sir Henry Tanner, father of the Hope Brothers' architect, and the President of the R.I.B.A., Sir Reginald Blomfield (1856–1942).

The Committee heard evidence from architects and tradesmen and reported in 1913. They came to

**Below** The Piccadilly Hotel and Quadrant, 1910.

JAMES THOMSON ARCHT

ON STONE BY T. G. DUTTON.

PERSPECTIVE VIEW OF THE INTERIOR OF THE GREAT GALLERY OF

THE POLYTECHNIC INSTITUTION,

*REGENT STREET. LONDON.*

*Plate XVIII*

Plate XIX

the conclusion that the Piccadilly Hotel should be made the centrepiece of a scheme modified as much as possible to meet the shopkeepers' objections without quarrelling too obviously with Shaw's design. In the new work the columns and arcades were to be abandoned, but the shop windows were still to be recessed behind the piers on the ground floor. The original lines of the main cornice and the string course above the mezzanine were to be kept, and the 'general style of character of the design should follow that of the hotel'.

The new design was to be adopted for the north side of the Quadrant, where, however, no attempt was to be made to repeat the effect of the Hotel as a central feature.

Discussions dragged on for another four years, matters being further delayed by being referred to the Cabinet. Finally, in 1916, it was agreed that Webb, Blomfield, and Ernest Newton, who had replaced Blomfield as President of the R.I.B.A. from 1914 to 1917, should collaborate on fresh designs for the Quadrant. This troika of talent was never really harnessed, perhaps fortunately for the artistic integrity of the new design, as well as for the speedy progress of the new buildings. It was Blomfield who was responsible for the new Quadrant, Piccadilly Circus and, to a large extent, for the atmosphere of the new Regent Street.

**Below** Norman Shaw's design for the Piccadilly Hotel and the Quadrant as displayed at the Royal Academy in 1906. **Bottom** Swan and Edgar's building before rebuilding in 1924. The large windows on the corner were put in in 1840, and much admired.

# New Regent Street

The report of the Committee was succeeded by the outbreak of the First World War, which further deferred rebuilding but also allowed tempers to cool. The world for which the Commissioners and their tenants finally rebuilt in the 1920s was a very different one from the leisured and wealthy world of Edwardian London.

Rebuilding at the south end of the street in Waterloo Place started with the bank on the corner of Pall Mall in 1902, and was followed in 1909 by the reconstruction of the insurance offices on the east side of the street. The new buildings were all in Portland Stone, and were more grandiose, and indeed altogether more monumental in scale. They followed Nash's original scheme in that the designs of the east and west sides matched exactly. The whole of Waterloo Place was not rebuilt until after the First World War but the Crown Commissioners seem to have met far less opposition from their tenants here, probably because they were largely prosperous banks and insurance companies who were not commercially inhibited by being asked to operate from Portland stone palaces.

Further up towards Piccadilly Circus rebuilding started with St Philip's Chapel in 1904, demolished for the building of Carlton House. No. 22 also seems to have been rebuilt early on to an obviously nineteenth century scale. It is now a slightly ridiculous but welcome anomaly in a street composed of massive inhuman stone blocks.

The rest of the street was rebuilt after the First World War, the south side of Piccadilly and Nash's

**Top right** The new Regent Street Polytechnic was designed by F.T. Verity in 1911.
**Below** Lower Regent Street from Waterloo Place about 1907.
**Bottom right** East Side of Waterloo Place in 1909, showing relative scales of old and new buildings.

GENERAL

old house, Nos. 14–16, surviving unaltered until then, as this nostalgic drawing by Hanslip Fletcher shows. Nash's house was replaced by Dorland House, which dwarfed Carlton Chambers, the last Nash building to survive on the east side of the street.

The row over 'Norman Shawism run mad'—the phrase was coined by a Swan and Edgar shareholder—had its permanent results in the way in which designs for the new buildings were adopted. Except in the sensitive area of the Quadrant and the Circus, where Blomfield was employed, the Commissioners were now prepared to consider schemes from tenants or groups of tenants for their sites, with the sole proviso that each block between streets should be rebuilt to a unified design.

These designs were submitted to John Murray, the Crown surveyor, who had the same responsibility for overall control of this new street as Nash had with the original street. However, he was in a much weaker position, and his only positive contribution to the design of the street seems to have been Edward VII Square, a proposal as French in its nomenclature as in its monumental scale. Nonetheless, his very long tenure of the post from 1904 until 1929 gave him considerable power, and all the designs were submitted to him for his advice and approval at some stage. If it was Arthur Cates, in a paper of 1898, who had laid down the strategy for the rebuilding, it was John Murray, holding court at the Carlton Hotel, who was responsible for the tactics—the architectural details which are so important to any streetscape. We are also indebted to Murray for the finest and most complete record of old Regent Street, the series of photographs commissioned from Bedford Lemere in 1910, of which a number have been used in this book. Just before his death, in 1940, Murray wrote a brief commentary on the series of photographs and on the changes in Regent Street during his tenure of office as Crown Surveyor.

Three new buildings were designed before Cates laid down his guidelines which included the idea of uniformity within the blocks and the use of Portland stone. This explains the rather aggressive design of Regent House, with its dome, and the use of mosaics on this building, and also that of red granite on the Robinson and Cleaver block (Nos. 156–170). Once the principle of uniformity within blocks was established, of course, it meant that the original design would be adhered to, however dated it might have appeared. A surprising number of the designs were indeed drawn up before 1912, though in most cases the whole block was not rebuilt until the 1920s.

Henry Tanner dominated the street above the Quadrant, being particularly important in the pre-war period. He rebuilt the whole of Oxford Circus, very typically, to a design made in 1912, and erected over a period of eleven years. He was also responsible for Nicoll's new block (Nos. 114 to 120) in 1912. After the war, he designed the new block for Dickins and Jones in 1921, and the new Chesham House (Nos. 132–154) in 1923. Opposite he designed another long block, Nos. 133–167, over an equally long time-span.

The longest block in the street was designed by F. T. Verity (1867–1937) the son of the great theatre architect, Thomas Verity (1837–1891), and like his father, trained in the French architectural tradition. This block, Nos. 161–201, between New Burlington Street and Conduit Street is much praised in a recent architectural assessment of Regent Street for its reconciliation 'of commercial

**Left** Paris House, part of Oxford Circus, rebuilt to the design of Henry Tanner. The Circus presented considerable problems because road widening in both Regent and Oxford Streets left only a segment of a circle, which combined with the greater height to reduce the feeling of a circus.
**Right** The new Robinson and Cleaver in 1910, the Ulster challenge to the Scottish block at Nos. 115–131 opposite. Because it was designed before the decision had been taken only to allow Portland stone, the façade was carried out in Swedish granite. One commentator thought that it was more like a pub or even a public building with its towers, suggesting 'anything but the fine fabrics sold within ...'

and aesthetic considerations' and the elegantly scaled result.

In many ways, of course, the design of a long block for a number of clients to a design that is neither miscellaneous nor so uniform as to be dull, is a much greater challenge than the design of a single block with a striking identity. It is part of the unfairness of life that it is the latter that are more remarkable and interesting. The only block built for a group of clients which is really noteworthy is Vigo House, where the architects Burnet and Tait repeated Nash's emphasis on the 'eye-catching' quality of the original domed block. Even this was more aggressively expressed in 1923 than 100 years before. The *British Builder* commented on the way in which the building jutted out 'into the Quadrant like the chin of a man who means business, and seems to express something of the character of the Scottish Architect who built it, or of the Scottish business for which it was built.'

More obviously striking are the two 'Beau Brummels of the West End'—Swan and Edgar's shop and the County Fire Office, 'which supports it as one gentleman should support another amongst a crowd of people who may be quite nice in their own way, but whose linen is sometimes a trifle doubtful'.

These buildings, both the work of Reginald Blomfield, guard the gateway to Regent Street in the way that Nash's buildings had done, though perhaps again more aggressively. Blomfield had converted Shaw's rusticated columns into rusticated

pilasters, which, taken with the long windows, owe more to the Second Empire than to Queen Anne. The new County Fire Office is very obviously a replacement in the new scale for the old, and very much more vertical in emphasis than the old, but otherwise attempts to make no new point. There had been a belated attempt to save the old building, clearly so distinguished a part of the old street, but this failed—perhaps indeed the old Fire Office would have been dwarfed into insignificance by the new Quadrant.

Swan and Edgar's department store is a totally new building in plan, in its relation to the rest of the Circus, and in its concept. It belongs, in many ways, to the generation of stores conceived before the First World War in imitation of Selfridges and Warings in Oxford Street. It gave a new control over the use of space for selling, and a new image as arresting as the traditional Swan and Edgar's corner. Like the rest of the new street, it was much higher, and this was emphasised by its strong vertical lines (Plate No. XXIII). It was a prodigy of building techniques in its rapid erection, and the way in which business was carried on alongside, and in some cases, over, both demolition and rebuilding processes. The building contractors, Higgs and Hill, prided themselves on the speed with which the contract was carried out, the excavation of the foundations for the new heavier steel-framed building being dug whilst business continued in the old one. The entire store was rebuilt in 1925–27, the last section on the Piccadilly frontage taking 25 weeks from commencement of building to the handing over of two floors for business.

**Left** The New County Fire Office designed by Blomfield, about 1927.

**Right** Swan and Edgar's new model gown department in the 1930s.
**Below** The County Fire Office, showing the stairs.
**Below right** Swan and Edgar, being rebuilt in August 1925.

Higgs and Hill carried out a number of jobs in Regent Street, including Dickins and Jones, Liberty's, and Aquascutum at No. 100 in the Quadrant, achieving great speed in several contracts. This was partly due to the practice of working at night by the light of flares.

Austin Reed, men's hosiers and tailors, were relative latecomers to Regent Street, Mr Reed having moved in 1911 from Fenchurch Street, where he had built up a successful shirt business. The new store was an interesting innovation since it was the first large men's store as such to be established in Regent Street, hitherto better known for its women's fashions.

The interior was planned and built by an architect called Brian Westwood, and had a variety of styles as wide, and as carefully organised, as those for the Piccadilly Hotel. Thus one bought an evening dress in a room with artificial light only, a made-to-measure suit in a Louis XV room, shoes in up-to-the-minute art deco, and tropical kit in a distinguished red lacquer room in a style reminiscent of Sezincote. For sporting clothes and dressing gowns, presumably intended for cold country houses, there were two floors of Tudor rooms. All this was swept away in the 1960s when the premises were reorganised in keeping with a less spacious age, together with the bathrooms and valeting service provided for customers in the basement.

Austin Reed, like a number of other stores, celebrated their re-opening with a luncheon. It took place at the Café Royal on October 25 1926, attended by a number of celebrities, including some of the well-known authors featured in their contemporary advertisements.

**Top left** Dickins and Jones being rebuilt in 1921.
**Centre left** Austin Reed: the Tudor staircase connecting the 4th and 5th floors.
**Bottom left** Austin Reed, Nos. 103–113 Regent Street. Tropical kit department, 1925
**Right** Austin Reed; Lift hall with lift gates designed by Joseph Emberton.

The Café Royal was also rebuilt, and though it did its best to maintain its old atmosphere by retaining the caryatids and the mirrors in the Grill Room, dating from the 1870s, Augustus John was not the only one to find the change disconcerting. Howard Robertson, in the *Architectural Review*, complained:

'. . . the Café Royal is no longer the likeable ne'er-do-well which we used to know. It no longer suggests the gaudy and smoky room which brought the boulevards to London, where Englishmen could enjoy the luxury of forgetting that they must always behave like Englishmen . . . But now it is reformed—not Royal, but Imperial; correct, reticent, discreet in both design and detail, dressed in black and the deepest bronze.'

Bronze was a material much favoured in the new Regent Street—for doors, fascias and often for fenestration; for the elegant lettering of the Austin Reed nameplate, featuring the firm's carefully designed symbol; for Ciro's shopwindow with its 'delicate and precious detail, complete "with French accent", and for the lamps outside Verrey's Café.'

The most striking individual new building was Liberty's new store built in 1925, which first brought the firm's many departments under a single roof. It is one of the most distinctive blocks in Regent Street, with its slightly concave front and the striking frieze on top with the figures leaning over. Few of us have time to look up when walking through Regent Street, which is a pity since there are a number of blocks which have been carefully placed to catch the eye, and none is more distinctive than Liberty's. It was designed by E. T. and E. S. Hall for Captain Stewart Liberty, the chairman of what is still very much a family firm, and a client with very definite ideas on design. The Regent Street shop windows were a long cry from the mogul shapes of the old East India House. They impressed one architectural writer nonetheless:

'The wares of both Orient and Occident looked well with their sober black framework, and the windows seem to have plate-glass of an almost luscious thickness and polish. [They] suggest a top-hatted and fur-coated wealth, a directorate courteous, polished, very English and patriotic, always open for business on the basis of quality, trust and confidence.'

All in all, despite the French influence of some of the architectural design, the new Regent Street does seem to have been a more national street, less haunted by 'moustachioed foreigners'. Perhaps English retailers had assimilated the lessons of the more cosmopolitan shopkeepers of Sala's day; possibly the new English flavour was due to the

emergence of a native fashion industry which was beginning to exploit the excellent home-produced materials, and the English reputation for good cut, particularly in men's wear.

If, however, a visitor to the new Regent Street proper found a stronger national flavour than before, when he turned the corner to newly widened Great Marlborough Street, he might well have thought he had stepped back into pre-Fire London.

**Left** The new Liberty's building, Nos. 208–222, in 1972.
**Below** Liberty and Co. workshops.
**Bottom** Liberty and Co., Great Marlborough Street building, in the 1920s.

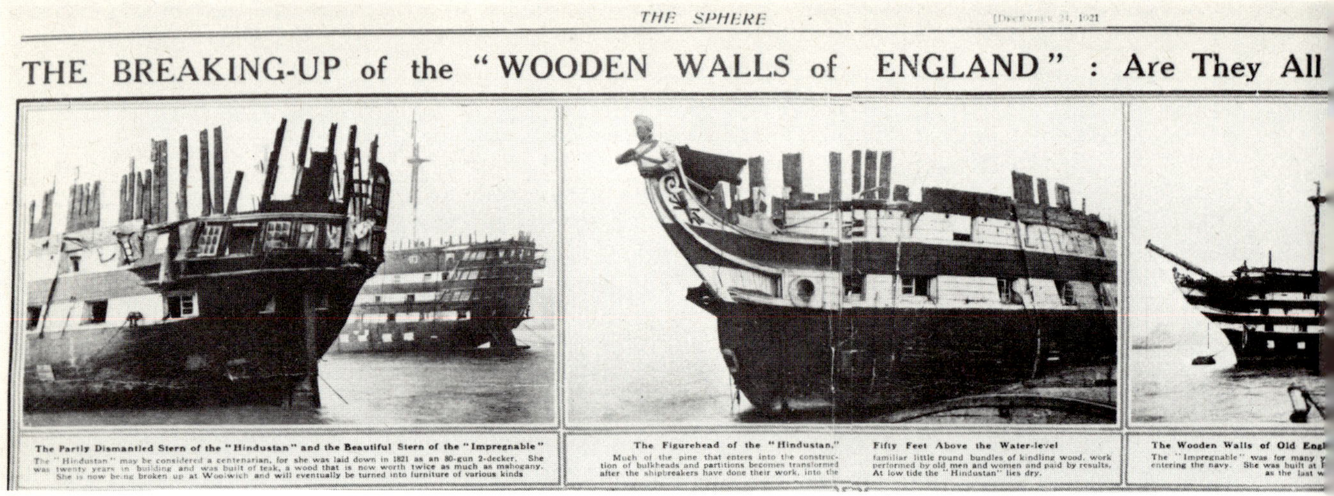

THE SPHERE [December 24, 1921

THE BREAKING-UP of the "WOODEN WALLS of ENGLAND" : Are They All

**The Partly Dismantled Stern of the "Hindustan" and the Beautiful Stern of the "Impregnable"**
The "Hindustan" may be considered a centenarian, for she was laid down in 1821 as an 80-gun 2-decker. She was twenty years in building and was built of teak, a wood that is now worth twice as much as mahogany. She is now being broken up at Woolwich and will eventually be turned into furniture of various kinds

**The Figurehead of the "Hindustan."**
Much of the pine that enters into the construction of bulkheads and partitions becomes transformed after the shipbreakers have done their work, into the

**Fifty Feet Above the Water-level**
familiar little round bundles of kindling wood, work performed by old men and women and paid by results. At low tide the "Hindustan" lies dry.

**The Wooden Walls of Old Engl**
The "Impregnable" was for many y entering the navy. She was built at as the last w

Captain Liberty, in a bout of opposition to the Crown Commissioners as vigorous as, but perhaps more constructive than that of Walter Morford, wanted to erect a new building, more English in character and more suitable in scale and atmosphere, for the display of their most important wares, furniture and interior decoration. It was constructed from the timbers of two old wooden ships, the H.M.S. *Hindustan* launched in 1824 during the completion of Nash's street, and H.M.S. *Impregnable* launched in 1865 and in her day the largest wooden ship afloat. The Portland stone used was chiselled, not sawn, the roofing tiles were hand made, the external timber mortised, tenoned and pegged, and the decorative external leadwork was also worked in the traditional way. This has given the building an integrity which has enabled it to survive the changes in artistic and architectural taste which have made other similar efforts in *pastiche* seem slightly ridiculous. The quality of the workmanship of the interior was equally impressive—woodwork, furniture and fitments were all designed and made in Liberty's own workshops—a tribute to the craftsmanship of the early twentieth century.

Taken all in all, architectural comment was mixed—the passing of the old street was bitterly resented and much deplored, not only by antiquarians but by the average Londoner. Much criticism had been levelled at the Commissioners for their decision to rebuild *in toto*, for the change to stone from the traditional London stucco, for the method used to arrive at a uniform design. In fact, they allowed more freedom to individual tenants and their architects than Nash had, partly perhaps because the twentieth century occupants of Regent Street had been there for a long time, and felt as proprietary about the street as did the Commissioners!

Interestingly enough, despite the greater freedom allowed, the new Regent Street struck at least one observer as more homogeneous:

'Because the distinctive individuality of the old Regent Street as a whole was so marked the absence of such a quality in the new is particularly manifest. The new street does not lack distinction: far from it: it is in fact one of the most distinguished of our streets. But it is a union not a unity, an aggregation of sumptuous and cleverly designed buildings rather than an apparently natural society of mutually interested units actuated by a single aim.'

o Disappear ? *Special "Sphere" Pictures.*

he "Impregnable" at Woolwich
training ship at Plymouth for boys
in 1860, and was the largest as well
ar-ship built

**Above** H.M.S. *Hindustan* and *Impregnable* at Woolwich, from the *Sphere* December 24 1924.
**Left** The demolition of No. 208 on the north side of Foubert's Place, from Conduit Street, drawn by Ian Strang in 1923.
**Right** Liberty and Co. The hall of the Tudor building: 'a Chinese puzzle conceived by a medieval mind'.

## 'The First Street in Europe . . .'

Rebuilding was a slow business and for many years Regent Street presented a curious appearance as some taller new blocks were interspersed with the old. The year 1923 saw the height of the post-war building boom, so much so that one cartoonist suggested that American tourists would get the impression that there had been a zeppelin raid. However, by 1927 most of the new buildings were completed and occupied, and the tradesmen had only the problem of welcoming back their old customers.

Regent Street shopkeepers always seem to have had considerable *esprit de corps*, and in 1927 they published *Regent Street: Past and Present*, an interesting piece of promotional material, more important for its picture of the rebuilt street than for its rosy memories of the past. Certain features of the old street survive in the new pattern of trade—corsetmakers are still important, since, as they point out, 'Youth is always in style'. Other prominent tradesmen include makers of boots and shoes—ready-made rather than bespoke—jewellers and watchmakers, furriers, and the growing number of houses dealing in men's fashions, and the elegant new Jay's, no longer a mourning warehouse. A modern note was struck by Electrolux, but their advertising car is no innovation—it is in the Regent Street tradition of Mr Perring's mobile hat! (see page 104).

The official opening took place in the summer of 1927, in a street more or less complete, sporting the proud declaration: 'The First Street in Europe welcomes the King and Queen'.

King George V and Queen Mary were due to attend the centenary celebrations of University College, and they were approached by the newly formed Regent Street Association to include the street in their route. It was kept a relatively modest affair and the royal couple were accompanied only by mounted servants and a handful of mounted policemen, and King George V, with typical royal consideration, asked that there should be no expensive decorations as he understood these were 'not consistent with the present condition of trade'. Only flags and bunting were permitted, but these were supplemented by lavish floral decorations. Over 20,000 blooms were used—roses, sweet peas, geraniums and clematis were all displayed, but pride of place was given to hydrangeas in the Queen's favourite shade of blue. These decorations were so much admired that the shopkeepers decided to leave them in place over the weekend so that those visitors who had not been able to watch the royal drive could still visit the street to see the flowers.

The royal opening took place on the afternoon of Thursday, June 23. This was the first official

**Below** Electrolux delivery van outside 155 Regent Street, in 1927.

royal visit to Regent Street since Queen Victoria drove through it in 1899, when she commented on Regent House, the first of the new generation of Regent Street buildings, which had then just been built to replace the Hanover Chapel. It was a small procession. The royal party was greeted by the Mayor of Westminster in Lower Regent Street and by the Mayor of St Marylebone in Upper Regent Street, to whom the King observed: 'I am very pleased with the new Regent Street, and I am glad to see it is nearly finished.'

On the whole, though press comment on the demolition of Nash's masterpiece had been very outspoken, others were also glad to see it was nearly finished.

'. . . this Regent-Street', decided the *Daily News*, 'is a better piece of work than it is painted by its critics. It improves undeniably on acquaintance. It possesses already a calm magnificence which it is difficult to quarrel with, and when time has weathered its Portland stone it will have lost that faint air of *nouveau riche* . . . Moreover, the new Regent-Street does in a sense typify the spirit of the age—in its vitality and brilliance and audacity. It is more suited to the flashing bus and the rapid streams of polished motorcars than to the old-fashioned coach-and-four. It is a part of changing London and changing England.'

**Below** The opening of Regent Street, June 23 1927. The royal procession driving up the Quadrant.

The public were very pleased with the new street, in which it was claimed that one could buy almost anything from a yacht or a dog to diamonds and pearls or a flawless complexion. Nonetheless, an American visitor was able to declare triumphantly that he had discovered a deficiency—there was no tobacconist. Not only was there no 'divan' complete with tobacco casks and sherry on tap presided over by some amiable successor to Mrs Carlin, but he had also found it impossible to buy cigarettes or matches anywhere in the street.

Perhaps the very last word on the new Regent Street should go to George Leveson-Gower, a Commissioner of Woods and Forests, one of the 'coterie of officials' who had to survive the brickbats and abuse of both shopkeepers and the press during the row over the Quadrant. Inevitably *The Times* had taken the opportunity to quote the famous quatrain about Nash which had appeared in the *Quarterly Review* for 1826, and which, in Sir John Summerson's words, 'has been quoted far, far too often':

'Augustus at Rome was for building renowned,
And of marble he left what of brick he had found;
But is not our Nash, too, a very great master?—
He finds us all brick and he leaves us all plaster.'

It is neatly annotated with the following conclusion:

'And with George Leveson-Gower still the process has grown,
As he found it all plaster and left it all stone!'

**Below** The new Swan and Edgar designed by Reginald Blomfield. The difference between the original Shaw windows and the revised Blomfield version is well shown, as is the lamentable difference in cleanliness between the new and old Portland stone.
**Top right** An advertisement from Hamley's catalogue.
**Bottom right** The Quadrant from Piccadilly Circus in October 1923, drawn by Hanslip Fletcher.

# HAMLEYS *For 1935* TRI-ANG *Children's Cars*

*These Children's Cars provide Healthy Exercise for all Boys and Girls*

## MARVEL

A realistic model of a light touring car with moulded steel body and opening door. Equipped with plated tubular bumper, dummy lamps and windscreen with direction indicator. Steel disc wheels with white jointless sponge rubber tyres. Length 35ins. Price **37/6**

## WHIPPET

The "Whippet" racing car has a polished aluminium body, and Magna type radiator. Complete with two dummy lamps, adjustable windscreen and direction indicator. White jointless sponge rubber tyres on direct spoke wheels. Length 36ins. Price **42/-**

*RING THE CHILDREN TO HEIR OWN MOTOR SHOW-OOMS ON THE FOURTH LOOR FOR A 'TRIAL RUN.'*

**TRI-ANG BRITISH-MADE TOYS.**

# V Regent Street

# since 1928

LONDON PAVILION
PAVILION
DEAN & DAWSON FOR TRAVEL
81 PICCADILLY W.1.
COCHRAN'S 1930 REVUE
ABDULLA SUPERB CIGARETTES
CHEMIST

## The founding of the Regent Street Association

'Regent-street . . . has certainly been for many months past the most talked of street in Europe. It has excited the fierce criticism of fastidious artists who loved the faded stucco and the serene proportions of the old Regent-street, and to whom the startling transfiguration in massive Portland stone is an unforgivable aesthetic outrage . . .'

Thus the *Daily News* summed up the twenty-five years of discussion and controversy over the rebuilding. For the shopkeepers it was now over, and the problem before them was to settle into their new premises in a period of increasing depression. The rebuilding had come at an unfortunate time—the actual construction had cost twice the pre-war figure, while the new leases had been granted in the post-war boom period. In the much quoted case of the wine merchants, Hedges and Butler, the original ground rent was £27.5s and that of the new lease £2000 per annum. This did not take into account the probable cost of their new building estimated at between £50,000 and £70,000. The increases throughout the street were comparable, leading to an overall rise from £44,000 in 1913, to £315,000 in the Crown's income from Regent Street ground rents. To the conservative eyes of the Regent Street tradesmen in the 1920s, without the experience of inflation that their successors were to enjoy, the increase was alarming; the recession of the late 1920s rapidly made it disastrous to some smaller firms. The peculiar difficulty of their position as Crown tenants was that they were dealing ultimately not with the Crown Commissioners but with the Treasury.

In 1925 a group of Regent Street shopkeepers had founded the Regent Street Association to help the tradesmen to deal with financial and other outstanding problems as a group. This corporate spirit had first been roused by the threat posed to Regent Street by Shaw's proposed 'dignified, cold, gloomy avenue of mausoleums'. It became properly organised to deal with the problems of the Depression, and it continued in existence in order to tackle the problems of visual amenity.

The Association first approached the Crown in 1928 on the question of the Regent Street ground rents, nearly three-quarters of which had been fixed since 1922. In 1934 negotiations were still proceeding, but with so little success that the Association suggested appealing to Parliament over the heads of the Treasury. The tenants felt that no private landlord would have been so obdurate, and that the Treasury was preventing the Crown Commissioners, who were relatively sympathetic, from renegotiating the rents. Complaints and negotiations continued – there were still a number of empty shops in Regent Street – throughout 1934. In December a deputation of M.P.s waited on the Crown Commissioners, but it was not until 1937, convinced by argument and the hard facts of the amount of rent arrears, that the Crown really agreed to negotiate. By 1938 these arrears were said to amount to over £225,000, one tenant owing £60,000, another £30,000. However, fairly speedy action was taken, once agreed, and the following year the First Commissioner could say, in answer to a Parliamentary question, that arrears were only

The interior of the Ford showrooms decorated for the Jubilee.

**Previous page** Piccadilly Circus in 1925

£133,000, of which £86,000 had been agreed. He added that the Crown was remitting rent to old tenants in need of relief.

However, the Association was not only concerned with the connected problems of ground rent and rates, it was also involved with the wider problems of Regent Street. It was the Association who invited King George V and Queen Mary to perform the opening ceremony in 1927, and who coordinated the decorations on that occasion. In 1934, with the worst days of the slump over, the nation was looking forward to the Jubilee celebrations. An imaginative scheme of flood-lighting the street was put forward, all the more dramatic because Regent Street was still gas-lit at the time. Though the occasion was the Jubilee, the object was to 'make Regent Street the most spectacular thoroughfare in the world'. It was intended to start in early autumn and to continue throughout four winters, lighting from 5.30 p.m. until midnight, except on Sundays.

For the Jubilee decorations themselves flowers were again to be used, and every individual business had its own display. A typical blend of loyalty and advertising was the Ford showrooms at No. 88, in the Quadrant. (See Plate No.XX) Of course, visitors flocked to London, and particularly to the West End. The *Daily Express* was not alone in its gloomy forecast of traffic jams – on May 3 1935 it published a picture of Regent Street solid with traffic to show the 'joys' of London to come.

Floral decorations, like floodlighting, became a feature of Regent Street. In 1936 the Association organised windowboxes throughout the street. In 1937 Regent Street was decorated for another royal event – the coronation of George VI – the first occasion on which a coronation procession had passed through the street, though it had been included in the routes of other royal processions.

## Difficulties and dangers: 1928-1945

Traffic was an increasing preoccupation in London. It was not only during a royal event that the streets were filled with angry drivers, as this happened in the normal course of life. The situation seems to have been exacerbated, however, by frequent road-mending. The laborious business of relaying tarred wooden blocks (only removed from Upper Regent Street in 1956), caused many of the 'Road Up' signs so lampooned in the 1920s and 1930s. Other repairs, concerned with gas, electricity, and sewage, also came in for comment.

The construction of the great concourse under Piccadilly Circus between 1925 and 1928 was therefore doubly welcome. It extended the Underground station serving the Piccadilly and Bakerloo lines, opened in 1906 to serve one and half million passengers a year, but totally inadequate for the 25 million expected by 1928. At the same time, the various public services which ran under the Circus were gathered into a single tunnel. This lessened the need to dig up the road every time there was any fault in any single one of them.

Eros was removed for the duration of the works, not without gratitude on the part of the authorities since the statue was always a liability during any kind of public occasion. The fountains could not be turned on without spraying passers-by, and the slender bow was often in danger from vandals. However, Eros was duly returned from a temporary exile in the Embankment Gardens on December 27 1931, and four days later, on New Year's Eve, the bow was damaged by a reveller who had climbed the statue. At the same time, new lamp standards were placed round the memorial and around Piccadilly Circus itself.

The famous Piccadilly flower-girls in their black straw hats and shawls had also been moved in 1925, and new pitches had been found for them: six took up positions round the Circus, two went east to Leicester Square, and two were found new stands near Park Lane. The Westminster Council did not want to renew their licences because of the traffic danger in an increasingly busy area, but were forced to do so.

In 1934 'safety lanes' controlled by police constables were introduced to safeguard the bewildered pedestrians, to the fury of the flower-girls who were condemned to 'isolation' with Eros. A 'gyratory system' for traffic had been introduced in 1926, to try and deal with the congestion from the seven streets meeting at Piccadilly Circus, again controlled by police constables. However, in 1937 an automated system of traffic lights, nicknamed 'Little Eva' was introduced to replace the thirteen constables. This was such an advanced system that Dr Todt, a German Inspector of Highways, in London on an official visit, was said to have stood for hours outside Swan and Edgar watching the traffic in admiration.

The traffic problems of Piccadilly affected Regent Street, and early in 1937, the Ministry of Transport proposed the banning of private cars waiting in Regent Street. It provoked a dignified objection from the Regent Street Association, who claimed that the street was wide enough for two fast lanes of through traffic, two slow lanes, and two rows of parked cars. Their reply revealed how important the chauffeur still was:

'The trade done by shoppers who come in their cars, and want them to wait while they are doing their shopping, is so great that any interference with this practice will be a serious blow . . .'

However, there were more serious blows ahead for Regent Street shopkeepers than those dealt by the Ministry of Transport. Goings-on in Piccadilly Circus provided an interesting index of popular preoccupations. In 1938, for instance, 300 Communists paraded in the Circus, and hung a white banner on Eros, saying 'Keep out Dr Ribbentrop', during the visit of the German Foreign Minister. A month later, in April, a counter demonstration of 1000 Fascist sympathisers was dispersed by mounted police.

In the summer of 1939 most people realised that war was inevitable and precautions against air raids began. In August the new dimmed lights were tried out and sandbags made their appearance, though Eros was not removed from Piccadilly Circus until the beginning of November, when his stand was boarded up for the duration.

The first bombs to explode in the Regent Street area were not German but Irish. On a Saturday evening in June 1939 six bombs were exploded in the area, including one near the Monico restaurant in Piccadilly Circus, and one in Sackville Street,

**Right** Broadcasting House and All Souls', Langham Place, about 1935. This somewhat distorted view shows the real elegance of the BBC's original building designed by Colonel Val Myer, and the BBC's Civil Engineer M.T. Tudsbury.
**Below** Christmas traffic in Regent Street in the 1930s.

just behind the Quadrant. A quarter of the advertising lights were put out and a great deal of glass was broken, but though there were some casualties, no-one was killed and no serious damage was caused. Police in the area were quickly on the scene, having commandeered taxis, full and empty, and ordered them to drive straight to the scene of the outrage.

The outbreak of war was in September 1939, but it was only in September 1940, a full year after the declaration of war, that bombs hit London. The raids began on September 7, first in daylight and then later on, at night, particularly when there was a full or 'bomber's moon'.

On September 18 a night bombing raid hit four major stores in Oxford Street and Oxford Circus, almost demolishing John Lewis on the north side of the street, damaging Selfridges, and Bourne and Hollingsworth, and knocking a great hole in the Oxford Circus front of Peter Robinson. A week later the newspapers reported that customers were being welcomed back by Bourne and Hollingsworth; that Peter Robinson had re-opened their eastern wing for business, though John Lewis were not yet ready to re-open – hardly surprising in view of the damage. The *Daily Mail* was able to reassure its readers that the accounts department 'had not been affected and monthly invoices would reach customers as usual.'

The Quadrant also suffered in September 1940. A large delayed-action bomb fell in the centre of Regent Street in the early hours of the morning, remaining on the surface, black and menacing. The street was cordoned off, the Piccadilly Hotel evacuated, and at daybreak the Royal Engineers arrived to deal with it. They used a method of steaming out the explosive under pressure, but unfortunately before the case was empty the fuse exploded — at 6.15 p.m. – in the middle of the evening rush-hour. Fortunately, the street was empty, and the bomb sandbagged, so no casualties resulted, but a good deal of expensive and indeed irreplaceable plate-glass was blown out of shop fronts up and down Regent Street, despite the special paper and the shatterproof sprays with which large plate-glass windows were treated. Even after a fortnight's bombing a routine had been established. Mollie Panter-Downes, a Londoner who visited Regent Street during the 'incident' described the routine – yellow tin police signs saying 'Diversion' and the crowds patiently watching the experts dealing with the lethal monster, cordoned off behind a rope. Police evacuated the nearby buildings, warning the owners to leave their windows open in the hope of preventing blast damage. Mollie Panter-Downes went to Regent Street the following morning:

'The scene next morning was quite extraordinarily eerie. The great sweep of Regent Street, deserted by everyone except police and salvage workers, stared gauntly like a thoroughfare in a dead city. It would have been no surprise to see grass growing up out of the pavements, which were covered instead with a fine, frosty glitter of powdered glass. The noise of glass being . . . swept into piles at street corners . . . made a curious grinding tinkle, which went on most of the day. The happiest people there were two little boys who had discovered a sweet shop where most of the window display had been blown into the gutter, and who were doing a fine looting job among the debris.'

The American *Time* magazine reported that 'Nash's Quadrant had been ripped by a bomb' – a report smartly contradicted by William Hickey, of the *Daily Express*, who pointed out that 'Nash's Quadrant' had been 'ripped' long since by the

**Below** Peter Robinson in 1942.

**Left** The premises of the Ford Motor Company in 1935 as decorated for the Silver Jubilee of King George V. The Ford Motor Company took No. 88 as their London headquarters and showrooms in 1933, when they moved their works to Dagenham. *Plate XX*

**Below** The interior of Hedges and Butler's shop at 155 Regent Street, about 1925. *Plate XXI*

**Left** The Duke of Beaufort Coach driven by the Marquis of Worcester, a noted amateur whip, starting from the Bull and Mouth Coach Office, Regent's Circus, Piccadilly, about 1841. *Plate XXII*

**Below** Swan and Edgar's new store. Design for rebuilding by Blomfield, from a perspective of 1925. *Plate XXIII*

housebreakers, and that the new Quadrant was 'not ripped at all considerably; if you walk up it, you see a certain number of chipped stones and gaping windows, the main structure intact'.

Regent Street's important position gave the 'incident' a considerable psychological importance, and Hickey emphasised that on the whole it was a 'cheering experience to visit Regent Street a fortnight after the Quadrant had, in the words of the pessimists, been completely wrecked. Traffic was running normally. Most of the shattered shops have reopened, though some of the windows have been replaced with planks with "Business as usual" and "Wet paint" on them, while others have resorted to the device of a small shop window with lots of wood.'

Such optimism was mandatory for journalists but the reality was horrifying, particularly for those who saw the cumulative damage unexpectedly. A prosperous housewife who went to look at Oxford Street that winter of 1940 wrote in her diary:
'It was the most ghastly sight imaginable. I had no notion that the empty charred skeleton with its blackened walls and gaping windows and rust-orange girders and its wax models lying like corpses on the pavement could look so terrible and forbidding . . . We stood dumbly staring at it in a sort of sick despair . . . Empty pavements and an empty silence through which the few pedestrians seemed to hurry furtively. Empty grey air, yet full of an oppressive feeling of desolation and despair . . .'

Her instinctive pre-war reaction was to collapse into a taxi, and to tell the driver to take her to the Café Royal. He drove down Regent Street, past the 'western curve . . . charred and pitted as high as the rooftops', but she found the Café Royal temporarily closed, having lost its windows in the bomb blast.

On the whole, however, morale among both West End store staff and their customers was remarkably high. The staff were dealing with the combination of bombing at work and bombing at home, living in dirt, dust and discomfort, and the difficulty of getting food and vital goods, particularly before strict rationing was introduced. Journeys home were often prolonged by raids, so closing hours were brought forward, but nothing could be done to ease the journeys into London through bombed railway junctions or in buses diverted down unfamiliar routes. Nonetheless, absenteeism was impressively low, even after the West End bombings of September 1940. Most large stores had public shelters in the basements, and when incendiaries became a serious menace fire-watching teams were organised to deal with the incendiary canisters.

**Below** The Quadrant in September 1940, after the explosion of a delayed-action bomb.

The motto was 'business as usual', with notices apologising to customers for the 'inconvenience' or directing them to a new address. Window displays continued in blasted windows, trading went on behind boarded-up façades, often with impromptu patriotic comment.

There were other problems for the shopkeepers – damaged stock could not be replaced from the dwindling supply at wholesalers and manufacturers; staff left to join the forces or to go into reserved occupations; and clothes rationing in the summer of 1941 put a moratorium on fashion for the time being, ushering in nearly a decade of austerity. Food rationing and controls on the price of meals affected hotels and restaurants, while the inevitable internment of foreigners removed large numbers of their staff.

At the top of Regent Street, Broadcasting House and its neighbours suffered a good deal of bomb damage. One of the most famous bombs fell during a news broadcast on December 8 1940, but a landmine that fell in Langham Place later that same night did a great deal more damage. The landmines used over London were very much heavier than ordinary bombs as they were naval magnetic mines rendered obsolete by advances in minesweeping techniques. The were parachuted down and this particular one drifted down into the roadway, caught on a lampost, and then exploded. It swept away four floors of the eastern bay of the Langham Hotel, including a bathroom in which someone was having a bath. The ghost of the unfortunate bather is still said to haunt the hotel, now used by the BBC as offices and staff bedrooms.

The Queen's Hall opposite survived the blast and indeed the rest of the winter's bombing, only succumbing to incendiary bombs on the last night of the Blitz, May 10 to 11, 1941. A fire bomb lodged where the firewatchers could not reach it in time, and they had to watch helplessly while the fire took hold and London's finest concert hall was burnt out. Henry Wood, who had pioneered the Promenade Concerts with Robert Newman at the Queen's Hall, is said to have wept when he saw the devastation. He conducted the last season of concerts there in 1940, only stopping the series in early September when it became impossible for audiences to get home in the blackout.

The girders from the balcony and circle, so well known to promenaders, together with the remains of the famous organ, went for scrap. The solid walls remained until the end of the war, as Chappell's, the sponsors for the concerts, planned to rebuild it. In the end, however, it was demolished and replaced by the St George's Hotel, opened in 1963.

These were some of the worst 'incidents' during the heaviest part of the bombing, the Blitz of

**Below** The Queen's Hall, Langham Place, wrecked by bombing in May 1941.

**Below** Piccadilly Circus in 1941.
**Right** Austin Reed advertisement of 1940.

the winter of 1940–1. There were other bombs, and later in 1944 and 1945 there were the V1s and V2s, one of which damaged the Regent Palace annexe in Brewer Street

The war saw the disappearance of a number of names in Regent Street, either 'for the duration' or for ever. Though men's tailors could turn to making uniforms, as did Austin Reed, who numbered Winston Churchill amongst their customers, it was more difficult for women's fashion shops to survive. One observer noted that it was the small businesses that could not compete; in any London shopping street 'you are likely to see shutters over the windows of dozens of modest businesses which struggled through the Blitz but could not survive clothes-rationing'.

The first indication that the war was coming to an end was the partial lifting of the blackout in September 1944, a small concession which had an enormous effect on morale. In December 1944, detachments of the Home Guard marched through Piccadilly as part of the stand-down ceremony. It was an event tinged with nostalgia as well as with gratitude that it was all almost over.

New Year's Eve 1944 was a more cheerful occasion than it had been for several years. It was attended by the traditional crowds in Piccadilly Circus as well as American servicemen.

Piccadilly Circus was, of course, the hub of the celebrations on the night that peace in Europe was declared. All roads into the Circus were closed to traffic, a bonfire blazed in the Haymarket, and singing and dancing went on all night, not only in the Circus, but even on top of a double decker bus!

## A new sort of shopkeeping . . .'

When Londoners looked at their city in the spring of 1945, they were appalled at the damage and decay. A correspondent wrote in the *Daily Express* of a grim 'Piccadilly-circus with black corrugated iron "hatches" covering the entrances to the Underground. Where Eros stood placards still urged the public to save. Famous advertisement signs are grimy and dim. The Clock on the great County Fire Office building presents a war-broken face without hands. . . . Regent Street is hazardous with wooden clamps covering pavement lights, relics of total blackout; clocks are dirty-faced and at a standstill hanging outside fashionable shops'.

It was going to be some time before the Circus was its usual garish self. The crowds seeing in the new year of 1946 had full street lighting, though they found themselves paying £3 15s for a bottle of whisky – a very considerable sum then. The following year the crowd was back to a pre-war 20,000, Eros returned in June to heavy rain and the enthusiastic welcome of two elderly flower-girls, who claimed to have sold flowers for more than fifty years.

In April 1949 the advertisements were lit up again for the first time since 1939. Large crowds of sightseers brought traffic to a halt in the Circus, an incontrovertible tribute to the public affection for the signs, which had been threatened by new powers of planning control which had been given to the Westminster City Council by new legislation. Serious discussion about the desirability of curbing the advertising had taken place, particularly as the London County Council had had several battles to limit the neon signs before the war. Orthodox town planning opinion was represented by Sir Patrick Abercrombie, who described Piccadilly Circus as 'a neon hell superimposed on a Blomfield heaven', a somewhat overstated case not shared by the public.

The Regent Street Association celebrated its 21st anniversary in 1947, a difficult time for celebrating anything in the midst of Crippsian austerity measures. However, it devised a 'Britain can make it' exhibition, an appropriate sequel to five years of 'Britain can take it'. This was an export drive to attract Commonwealth and American visitors, for whose benefit they arranged with the Treasury a special relaxation of currency control. The austere decorations featured a set of scales – for balance of payments – still a familiar motif, and they were designed by Mrs Jill Greenwood, a designer who was to be responsible for a number of Regent Street schemes. The *Manchester Guardian* found the decorations:

'a pleasant blend of discipline and indiscipline . . . In these days it is good to see shopkeepers exerting themselves so; it shows that if the shops are short of commodities their owners are not without imagination and ambition.'

The following year the Association put up Christmas trees throughout the street, but was forbidden to light them. In 1949 lighting restrictions were off, and the Christmas trees were lit up. It was not till 1954, following the successful Coronation decorations, that the first full-scale Regent Street Christmas lights went on, and only then after considerable opposition from the Westminster and St Marylebone City Councils who were worried about safety.

By 1955 the Christmas lights were a matter of tradition, as the *Evening News* declared:

'The annual glittering display running down Regent Street has become the Christmas pride of London. Tourists are delighted with it . . . It is being televised in the United States. Thousands come to gaze at the colourful sparkle every night . . .'

The visit to the West End to see the Christmas decorations was an annual joy for Londoners for over fifteen years, until in the 1970s growing concern about fuel and power resources made such a display increasingly difficult to stage.

The idea of cooperation had grown during the war, when firms delivered each other's parcels, arranged to decorate the windows of empty premises in the street, and shared the use of shelters. In the difficult post-war years the concept and work of the Regent Street Association grew – ingenuity had to compensate for lack of resources. In 1950 the London art schools were offered the opportunity to dress the Regent Street windows for a week – the prize was won by the Royal College of Art team with the theme 'Bull in a China Shop'. In 1952 an annual spring window dressing competition was instituted, and of course throughout the 1950s, the

**Top** The lights go on again in Piccadilly Circus, in April 1949.
**Left** The Christmas decorations in 1960, looking up Regent Street.
**Above** Christmas 1971. Putting up the lights in Regent Street.

Christmas lights became more ambitious in scope and design, then in the imaginative hands of Beverley Pick and Mrs Jill Greenwood.

This coordination was not achieved without effort, and in 1955 the *Daily Mail* identified the source of much of the drive – the secretary of the Association, Mrs Martin Gray. She had been secretary since 1948, 'a busy little sergeant-major who makes sure that those privileged to own shops and businesses in that street have a proper sense of their responsibilities. They call her "Mrs Regent Steet" and hold her in awe.' Amongst her duties, the article added, was 'flag discipline', which was very strict. Attendance at the street's luncheon club and at its golf society was also officially encouraged, where members could 'exchange views and be generally chummy with other Regent-streeters'.

The problems facing the post-war generation of shopkeepers in Regent Street were different not only in scale but also in kind from those confronting their forerunners. People still come to Regent Street to shop, but no longer only, like Sala's 'ladyship', from a West End mansion or indeed from 'the suburbs and the country' as in Edwardian times, but from all over the world. Regent Street has shared in the London tourist boom, and this inevitably has changed the emphasis from foreign fashions purveyed to the Londoner, to the sale of the best of British design and make to the foreign visitor to London.

The character of the Regent Street shops has changed somewhat since the beginning of the century. There are now as many shops concerned with masculine fashion as with feminine – a change which gives the lie to a suggestion made by a German journalist in the 1930s that streets primarily for women ran north and south, while those in which men did their shopping ran east to west! The big department stores – Liberty's, Peter Robinson, and Dickins and Jones all have men's departments, while there are a number of internationally known men's shops. Some like Airey and Wheeler or Aquascutum have been in Regent Street since the last century, others like Austin Reed or Acuman, were established elsewhere before moving to premises in Regent Street.

The changing pattern of retailing is reflected too in the number of fashion specialists, both in men's and women's clothing, and many shoe retailers, in particular, find a shop in Regent Street a necessity. Richard Shops and Miss Selfridge are two of the women's fashion experts, while men are catered for by such firms as Harry Fenton, Dunns, Montague Burton, and the Village Gate. The Scotch warehouse tradition lives on in the premises of the Scotch House, who deal in all kinds of Scottish artefacts, not only in fabrics.

Jewellery has always been well represented, though today the same tendency towards larger organisations can be seen in the jewellery trade as elsewhere. There are still, however, a number of firms who have had premises in the street since mid-Victorian times, such as Packer and Company, and T. & J. Perry, established at No. 226 in 1862.

Carrington and Company were started by Sir Edward Thomason, a former partner with Boulton and Watt in Birmingham, who invented a 'close-plating' process for ferrous metals in 1810. A Mr Collis took the firm over in 1848, and it became Carrington's in the 1890s. Though primarily silversmiths and electroplaters, the firm also worked as jewellers to Queen Victoria for whom they made a necklace in 1887, thus earning a royal warrant. They also made the crown worn by Queen

Alexandra at the coronation of Edward VII in 1902.

At the other end of the same block, at No. 112, were the Goldsmiths and Silversmiths' Company, established in the 1890s, and dealing in fine furniture as well as in silver. In 1952 they amalgamated with Garrards, the Crown Jewellers, who moved from Albemarle to Regent Street. Garrards started in the Haymarket in the middle of the eighteenth century. The first member of the Garrard family joined the firm in 1796, and it remained a family firm for 150 years. A Garrard was appointed Crown Jeweller in 1840 and a member of the firm has held the appointment ever since. They cut the Koh-i-Noor diamond for use in the Crown jewels and they have made a number of royal crowns for special occasions, including coronations, and one for Queen Mary for the Delhi durbar of 1911.

Perhaps the largest jeweller in Regent Street is Mappin and Webb, who took over Savory and Moore's premises at No. 220 in the 1870s. The founder Jonathan Mappin came from Sheffield, and the firm started as wholesale cutlers. In 1915 they built elegant new premises at No. 172 to the design of J. J. Joass, next door to the more ebullient premises of Robinson and Cleaver. 'This quiet and reticent' new building carried on the tradition of sensitive architectural patronage, established by the firm's dramatic headquarters in Oxford Street, erected in 1906–08, again to the design of Belcher and Joass.

The status of shop assistants has also changed since Charles Booth's day when they worked a six-day week of some 65 or 70 hours. Now the five-day week is almost universal for administrative staff, and though sales staff work on Saturdays as well, this is now on a shift basis. An interesting development in the last decade has been the development of Saturday as an important shopping day in the West End. Saturday afternoon and even whole day closing made its appearance in the late 1950s and 1960s, but it is probably true to say that Saturday is now universally recognised as a day for leisured family shopping. An additional incentive for the West End shops are the theatre and cinema audiences who can be tempted up a little early to take in some shopping before the show.

Late night shopping on one night a week was begun in Regent Street in 1951 for the Festival of Britain, but the permanent adoption of this later opening required changes in legislation. This has now been achieved, and the 7 or 8 p.m. late opening on Thursdays now brings a regular flood of shoppers up from the suburbs, and enables people working in London to take advantage of its superior shops before catching their trains home. Seven was the average evening winter closing time for West End shops in the 1890s, with an hour later in summer, though shop assistants then started their day even earlier. Certain West End closing hours have become much earlier—the night life of Piccadilly Circus, and the area round about seems never to have recovered from the blackout.

This shift in hours is one of the responses made by Regent Street shopkeepers to the change in national habits, since the Second World War. This provided a complex and difficult challenge well summed up by Captain Stewart Liberty, President of the Regent Street Association and head of one of the few family businesses left in Regent Street. He wrote in response to criticism to the *Daily Telegraph* in 1954:

'The national income is spread more equally over the population than in the eighteenth century. Regent Street, among other shopping centres, now has to cater for a very large proportion of this population, whereas in the days of Nash it catered for a relatively small, wealthy and cultured section of society.

'The small specialised shops of the past, with their very personal service, are unhappily disappearing. But a new sort of shopkeeping is emerging, calling for new techniques . . . the science of shopkeeping is now studied with more seriousness and vigour than ever.'

**Left** The east side of Regent Street in 1951.
**Below** Regent Street looking south from Oxford Circus in 1971.

## Neon hell' or 'Blomfield heaven'?

Physical changes in the area of Regent Street between the two circuses have been relatively few since the war. This is perhaps a belated tribute to the real physical need for rebuilding Nash's street; undoubtedly the Portland stone structures with their steel skeletons stood up a great deal better to high explosive or incendiary bombs than the Georgian brick and timber would have done. Shop fronts have changed—as Nash recognised, a flexible shop front is the first requirement of a shopkeeper—but they have remained more sober than those in neighbouring Carnaby Street.

In Lower Regent Street a number of changes have taken place. Here the last Nash houses disappeared only in 1939, when No. 11 was demolished. Together with No. 11 went Nos. 5–9, the premises of Howell and James, silk mercers and jewellers, which had been reconstructed for them in 1881 with a new terracotta façade. The new building by Wimperis and partners was not erected till 1951. It strikes a courteous and congruous note between Carlton House, erected on the site of St Philip's Chapel in 1904, and British Columbia House, built about ten years later. This last was given a bay window to echo that of the United Service Club across the street, a now obsolete courtesy since the Club itself has disappeared. The new building for the United Kingdom Energy Authority, by Trehearne and Norman (1955–8), is neither distinguished in a contemporary style, nor a piece of graceful *pastiche*. Altogether the east side of Lower Regent Street makes one very grateful for the Commissioners' insistence that Blomfield's design should be carried out all round Piccadilly Circus.

Piccadilly Circus now reminds the visitor of the joke about the Holy Roman Empire—it has not been a Circus since 1885, and it is in many ways no longer part of either Piccadilly or Regent Street. In Nash's scheme it was an elegant way of joining two important streets physically and psychologically. It is now a living example of urban decay, unattractive to the average pedestrian and an inconvenient form of roundabout to the car driver.

To state the unpleasant facts thus crudely is not to underestimate the problems or indeed the amount of talent and goodwill which has been devoted to solving this difficult problem now

**Left** The Regent Street area from the air, 1968.
**Top** West side of Regent Street in 1964.
**Above** The west side of Lower Regent Street in 1971.

ninety years old. Nor is this the place to examine the options or to discuss the problems on which developers, town planners, traffic experts—and Londoners—have to agree.

The problem was first posed for Londoners in October 1958 when the London County Council mounted an exhibition showing a proposal for the Circus by a group of developers. This foresaw redevelopment in three stages, first the Monico site, which was intended to be completed by 1965, followed by that of the London Pavilion. Finally, was to be the redevelopment of the Criterion block, which was to be linked to the new traffic scheme making Jermyn Street between the Haymarket and Lower Regent Street part of the Piccadilly traffic system. This exhibition provoked a number of complaints some of which were met by the redesigning of the Monico tower in the following year. It also provoked a dignified rebuke from Austin Blomfield, who suggested that his father's schemes should be completed, urging that Piccadilly Circus:

'surely . . . deserves a uniform and regular treatment in the grand manner, rather than an assemblage of different designs and character competing with each other.'

A number of schemes have since been put forward to meet this and other *desiderata* by some of the best known names in British architecture and town planning. These have included a pedestrian walkway, roofing the circus over, putting the traffic underground – the whole gamut indeed of contemporary solutions to difficult town planning problems. The recently increased interest in Victorian architecture which has led to the revaluing of the Criterion, the 'best surviving building of Thomas Verity', will not make the town planners' task any easier.

It would be rash to forecast the outcome of the latest batch of planning proposals. One can only hope that Piccadilly will still keep its place as the heart of any London celebration. For the Victorians it was *the* place to celebrate Boat Race night, Derby Day, and national victories, in such an uninhibited fashion that it is said that the mounted police cleared the bar at the Criterion on horseback. Their children and grandchildren celebrated the peace of 1918 and that of 1945 in Piccadilly Circus. In 1949, when the advertisements were switched on again, some 50,000 people went there to welcome back the lights.

The average Londoner's brief for Piccadilly Circus was well summed up by a London County Councillor in 1958, and so far it has proved difficult to meet:

'We want Piccadilly Circus to be gay, light, if you like, untidy, but above all cheerful, with a sense of freedom even if that freedom goes a little too far on Boat Race night. Piccadilly Circus is a beautiful mess. The trouble about town planners is that they cannot abide beautiful messes.'

To reconcile that *cri de coeur* with Austin Blomfield's rebuke, the needs of traffic, the demands of Victorian enthusiasts, and the expectations of developers, will be no easy task. It will take the feeling for townscape, the architectural ingenuity, the diplomacy and the commercial acumen of another John Nash. Let us hope these qualities are found since Piccadilly Circus is such a key point in his scheme that its disgraceful condition damages the whole length of his New Street. It would be a cause for congratulation if in 1975 – the 150th anniversary of Regent Street's completion – a permanent solution to the central problem of Piccadilly Circus could be found.

**Left** Swan and Edgar in 1971.

**Above** County Fire Office in Piccadilly Circus in 1971.

The new Regent Street on completion in 1927 looking south towards the Piccadilly Hotel. This view shows the uncluttered elegance of the rebuilt Quadrant, and the way in which the Aquascutum building echoes the curve of the north side. Though the buildings are no longer those of John Nash, his original concept lives on in the curving façades and the uniform treatment of the new frontages.

# List of picture sources

The author and publishers gratefully acknowledge the help of all those who have lent photographs and given permission for their reproduction in this book. For brevity the main sources of illustrations have been abbreviated as follows:

| | |
|---|---|
| GLC | Greater London Council |
| GLC (MC) | Greater London Council Map Collection |
| GLC (PC) | Greater London Council Print Collection |
| GLC (PL) | Greater London Council Photograph Library |
| G | Guildhall Library, City of London |
| T | The Tate Gallery, London |
| WCL | The Archives Department, Westminster City Libraries (for both Marylebone and Victoria Library) |
| BM | British Museum |
| NPG | National Portrait Gallery, London |
| K | Kodak Museum |
| NMR | National Monuments Record (Crown Copyright). Suffix (BL) indicates a photograph by Bedford Lemere |
| RTHPL | Radio Times Hulton Picture Library |
| RIBA | Royal Institute of British Architects, Drawing Collection |

**Black and white illustrations:**
**End papers from** *Grand Architectural Panorama of London: Regent Street to Westminster Abbey* by R. Sandeman and G.C. Leighton, published in 1849 by I. Whitelaw, London and reproduced in 1966 by Edward Stanford Ltd. (No. 105 London Topographical Society)
*front* Waterloo Place and Lower Regent Street
*back* Lower Regent Street and part of the Quadrant

**Frontispiece** The Wallace Collection, London
**page 10** *Metropolitan Improvements*

I METROPOLITAN IMPROVEMENTS
**page 12–13,** *Metropolitan Improvements* **14, 15,** WCL **16** BM (Crace Collection) **17** BM (Crace Collection) **18** WCL **21** top GLC bottom Jesus College, Oxford **22** BM **23** GLC **24, 25,** BM (Crace Collection).

II THE CREATION OF REGENT STREET
**page 26–27,** *Metropolitan Improvements* **29** top WCL bottom BM (Crace Collection) **30** BM **31** GLC **32** BM (Crace Collection) **33** BM **34–35,** top BM (Crace Collection) bottom BM **37** *Metropolitan Improvements* **38** top BM (Crace Collection) bottom *Metropolitan Improvements* **39** top *Metropolitan Improvements* bottom WCL **40** top BM (Crace Collection) bottom BM (Crace Collection) **42** GLC (PC) **43** top GLC (PC) bottom BM (Crace Collection) **44** RIBA **45** top GLC (PL) bottom GLC (PC) **46** GLC (PC) **47** NMR **48, 49,** BM (Crace Collection) **50** left BM (Crace Collection) right Swan and Edgar **51** G **53** GLC (PL) **54, 55,** *Metropolitan Improvements* **56** GLC (PC) **57** top BM (Crace Collection) bottom G **58** *Metropolitan Improvements* **59** top NMR bottom G **60, 61, 62, 63, 64, 65, 66, 67, 68, 69,** Tallis: *London Street Views*

III THE ONLY BOULEVARD IN LONDON
**page 70–71,** GLC 73 top NMR bottom *Illustrated London News:* GLC (PC) 76, 77, 78, 79, 80, 81, 82, NMR 83 top NMR middle K 84 K 85 top Illustrated Newspaper Group (LEA Dept.) bottom *Illustrated London News* 86 NMR (BL) 87 WCL 88 top NMR (BL) bottom NMR 89 NMR 90 left NMR (BL) right Verrey's Ltd. 91 GLC (PL) 92 BM (Map Dept.) 93 NMR 94 Hedges and Butler 95 G 96 top NMR (BL) bottom Liberty and Co. 97 top and left Liberty and Co. right Dickins and Jones 98 top NMR bottom *The Sphere* 99, 100, 101, NMR 102 *Country Life* 103 top NMR bottom WCL 104 top *Country Life* bottom Charles Knight: London 105 top Aquascutum bottom GLC (PL) 106 top NMR (BL) middle Jaeger and Co. bottom International Fur Company 107 top Jaeger and Co. bottom Lillywhite and Co. 109 top *Illustrated London News* bottom G 110, 111, G.

IV THE REBUILDING OF REGENT STREET: 1904–1928
**page 112–113,** GLC (PL) 115 top GLC (PL) bottom NMR 116 NMR 117 Crown Estate 118 top NMR bottom Crown Estate 119, 120, NMR 121 top NMR bottom Swan and Edgar 122 GLC 123 top NMR bottom right GLC 124 NMR 125 NMR (BL) 126 NMR 127 top Swan and Edgar bottom left *Architectural Review* bottom right Higgs and Hill 128 top Higgs and Hill middle Austin Reed bottom Austin Reed 129 Austin Reed 130 NMR 131 top Higgs and Hill bottom Liberty and Co. 132 top *The Sphere* bottom G 133 NMR 134 *Regent Street: Past and Present* 135 *The Times* 136 Swan and Edgar 137 top Hamleys bottom G

V REGENT STREET SINCE 1928
**page 138–139,** WCL 140, 141, Ford Motor Co. 143 top NMR bottom *The Times* 144 Imperial War Museum 145 Associated Press 146 left Architectural Press right Imperial War Museum 147 Austin Reed 149 top *Daily Express* bottom left Sport and General Press Agency Ltd. bottom right *The Times* 150, 151, GLC 152 Aerofilms 153, 154, 155, GLC 156, RTH PL

**Colour illustrations:**
**Front cover** See Plate XII **Back cover** See Plate XX
**Plate I** The Little Theatre GLC **Plate II** The King's Theatre GLC **Plate III** The New Street looking towards the Quadrant GLC **Plate IV** Langham Place and Portland Place GLC **Plate V** East Crescent, now part of Park Crescent BM (Crace Collection) **Plate VI** Regent Street looking north from Hanover Chapel to All Souls' Langham Place GLC **Plate VII** St James's Market about 1840 GLC **Plate VIII** Nash cartoon 1824 BM (Crace Collection) **Plate IX** Plan of the New Street BM (Crace Collection) **Plate X** View from Regent Circus (Piccadilly) south to Carlton House BM (Crace Collection) **Plate XI** Waterloo Place BM (Crace Collection) **Plate XII** *(also front cover)* Regent Street looking south from the Hanover Chapel in 1842 G **Plate XIII** The Prince Regent G **Plate XIV** The Quadrant 1822 G **Plate XV** The Quadrant 1852 G **Plate XVI** Cumberland Terrace 1836 WCL **Plate XVII** The Colosseum 1836 WCL **Plate XVIII** The Polytechnic Institution G **Plate XIX** Café Royal T **Plate XX** *(and back cover)* Ford Motor Company 1935 Ford Motor Company **Plate XXI** Hedges and Butler in 1925 Hedges and Butler **Plate XXII** The Duke of Beaufort Coach G **Plate XXIII** Swan and Edgar in 1925 Swan and Edgar

# Bibliography

Adburgham, A. *Shops and shopping* (1964) Allen and Unwin
*Architectural Review 1927* pp. 202–239, series of articles on rebuilt Regent Street
Beerbohm, Max *Yet Again* (1909) Chapman and Hall
Clunn, Harold *London Rebuilt, 1897–1927* (1927) Murray
*The Face of London* (1934) Simpkin Marshall
Davis, Dorothy *A History of Shopping* (1966) Routledge and Kegan Paul
Davis, Terence *John Nash, The Prince Regent's Architect* (1966) Country Life
Deghy, G. and Waterhouse, K. *Café Royal: Ninety Years of Bohemia* (1955) Hutchinson
Edwards, A. Trystan *Good and Bad Manners in Architecture* (1946) Tiranti
Elmes, James *Metropolitan Improvements; or, London in the Nineteenth Century* (1827) Jones and Co.
Knight, Charles *London* (1843) Charles Knight
London County Council *Survey of London* Vols. XX, XXIX, XXX, XXXI, XXXII
Mosley, Leonard *Backs to the Wall* (1971) Weidenfeld and Nicolson
Panter-Downes, Mollie *London War Notes* (1972) Penguin Books
Saunders, Ann *Regent's Park* (1969) David and Charles
Sansom, William *Westminster in War* (1947) Faber
Sala, G.A. *Twice Round the Clock* (1859) Houlston and Wright; *Gaslight and Daylight* (1859) Chapman and Hall *London Up to Date* (1894) Adam and Charles Black
Sekon, H.A. *Locomotion in Victorian London* (1938) Oxford University Press
Summerson, John *John Nash, Architect to King George IV* (1935) Allen and Unwin; *Georgian London* (1945) Pleiades Books
Tallis, John *London Street Views 1838–1840* (1969) Nattali and Maurice
Walford and Thornbury *Old and New London* (n.d.) Cassell

# Index

*Page numbers in bold indicate where there is also an illustration or caption reference:*